BUILT ON COMMI

Liverpool's central business district

Published by English Heritage, Kemble Drive, Swindon SN2 2GZ
www.english-heritage.org.uk
English Heritage is the Government's statutory adviser on all aspects of the historic environment.

© English Heritage 2008

Printing 10 9 8 7 6 5 4 3 2 1

Images (except as otherwise shown) © English Heritage, © English Heritage. NMR or © Crown copyright. NMR.

First published 2008

ISBN 978 1 905624 34 8
Product code 51331

Liverpool Vision has made a financial contribution towards the publication of this book.

British Library Cataloguing in Publication Data
A CIP catalogue record for this book is available from the British Library.

Application for the reproduction of images should be made to the National Monuments Record. Every effort has been made to trace the copyright holders and we apologise in advance for any unintentional omissions, which we would be pleased to correct in any subsequent edition of this book.

The National Monuments Record is the public archive of English Heritage. For more information, contact NMR Enquiry and Research Services, National Monuments Record Centre, Kemble Drive, Swindon SN2 2GZ; telephone (01793) 414600.

Brought to publication by Rachel Howard, Publishing, English Heritage.
Edited by Swales & Willis Ltd, Exeter.
Page layout by Swales & Willis Ltd, Exeter.
Printed in the UK by Cambridge Printing.

Front cover
Commercial palaces of Castle Street. The former Adelphi Bank, 1891–2, is on the left; the former Leyland & Bullin's Bank, 1895, on the right. Behind them rises India Buildings, 1923–30.
[AA029367]

Inside front cover
The commercial centre seen from the tower of the Municipal Buildings, looking along Dale Street towards the Pier Head.
[AA030720]

BUILT ON COMMERCE

Liverpool's central business district

Joseph Sharples and John Stonard

The City of Liverpool

ENGLISH HERITAGE

Contents

Frontispiece
*Sir Thomas Street from the tower of the
Municipal Buildings, showing the dense
grain of the commercial centre.*
[AA030717]

Acknowledgements

The authors would like to thank the following for their help in the preparation of this book: Chris Griffiths, John Hinchliffe, Glynn Marsden and Wendy Morgan of Liverpool City Council; John Cattell, Colum Giles, Adam Menuge, Louise O'Brien and the late Ian Goodall of English Heritage; and Adrian Jarvis, Robert Lee, Sari Mäenpää, Graeme Milne, Kati Nurmi and John Siddell of the University of Liverpool. The photographs were taken by Keith Buck, James O Davies, Tony Perry and Bob Skingle, and Allan Adams drew the graphics. Iain Black made many useful comments on the text. We are also grateful to the staff of the Liverpool Record Office, the Lancashire Record Office and Liverpool University Library, and to owners who have allowed access to their buildings. Figures 47, 49b, 50 and 58 are based on drawings in the Culshaw and Sumners papers held by the Lancashire Record Office, and are reproduced with the consent of Edmund Kirby & Sons, India Buildings, Liverpool. Figure 49e is based on a drawing in the possession of the Naylor Trust. The book is an outcome of the University of Liverpool's Mercantile Liverpool Project, jointly funded by the Leverhulme Trust and English Heritage, with support from the Philip Holt Trust and Liverpool City Council's World Heritage Site.

Foreword

Liverpool is pre-eminently a commercial city. In its period of greatness as a trading port, it only existed to promote business and the movement of goods. It was this that made it, after London, the nation's and the British Empire's leading port. As such, its appearance today is dominated by reminders of the traffic and business of trade. Perhaps most obviously, the docks and warehouses show us where goods were landed and stored. But the city's historic commercial centre was where the deals were done, where trade was financed and insured, where money was made, and it is here that Liverpool still shows its global importance and the source of its wealth.

This historic central business district forms a vital part of Liverpool's character and the centrepiece of the World Heritage Site. The value of this distinctive environment is being recognised today in more than cultural terms, for its quality attracts inward investment and provides the city with a special identity, a precious commodity in a world which is increasingly uniform. The commercial district is a dynamic place and requires careful management. To survive as an area that contributes to the quality of life in the city, the district must adapt to accommodate new uses and new ways of organising life and work. Successful development will depend upon a good understanding of distinct historic character, on an appreciation of the contribution which this makes to people's lives and perceptions of place, and on the physical requirements of modern buildings.

This book seeks to provide some of that understanding, to open up the enjoyment of this unique environment to a wide audience, and to demonstrate that sensitive handling of change is vital for Liverpool's future and for the continuing success of its commercial core. The partners within the Historic Environment of Liverpool Project – English Heritage, Liverpool City Council and Liverpool Vision – are committed to this objective.

Lord Bruce-Lockhart, Chairman, English Heritage
Councillor Warren Bradley, Leader, Liverpool City Council
Sir Joe Dwyer, Chairman, Liverpool Vision

CHAPTER 1

The development of the business district

Among the great cities of the world ... there is no other so exclusively devoted to commerce. Every house in Liverpool is either a counting-house, a warehouse, a shop, or a house that in one way or other is either an instrument or the result of trade ... and the inhabitants are nearly to a man traders or the servants of traders.

J G Kohl 1844[1]

Liverpool is a city built on trade. It was the potential of its natural harbour – the Pool – that led King John to make it a borough in 1207, and maritime trade was the source of its success for much of the next 700 years. Coastal, Irish and European shipping were joined in the 17th century by trade with the American colonies, and in the 18th century by the ignominious but lucrative slave trade. Liverpool reached the height of its wealth and prosperity in the 19th and early 20th centuries, when it became the chief *entrepôt* for industrial Britain and the rest of the world. International and imperial trading ties are celebrated in the names of office blocks such as the Pekin and Kansas buildings (Figs 1 and 2), in

Figure 1 *Detail of façade of Pekin Buildings, Harrington Street, c1859. [DP28725]*

Figure 2 *Detail of façade of Kansas Buildings, Stanley Street, 1890s. [DP28706]*

the sculptural decoration of Union House and the Cunard Building (Fig 3 and back cover), and in the stained-glass windows of the magnificent Mersey Docks and Harbour Board offices (now the Port of Liverpool Building), which depict the coats of arms of Britain's colonies and dominions (Fig 4).

The port's role as a distribution centre of global reach was vividly described by the journalist William Allingham in 1870

Figure 3 *Chinese workers handling tea: detail of frieze in Union House, Victoria Street, 1882. [DP28846]*

> Hither converge in ceaseless streams the cotton of America, India, Egypt, the wool of the Australian plains, the elephants' tusks and palm oil of African forests, the spermaceti of Arctic seas, the grain from the shores of Mississippi, St. Lawrence, Elbe, Loire, Danube, Vistula, and many another stream, the hides of South America, the sugar, copper, tobacco, rice, timber, guano, &c., of every land the sun's eye looks upon. Hence radiate to all quarters of the globe, bales of cotton goods, linen, woollen,

Figure 4 *Stained glass with the arms of Australia, by G Wragge & Co, Port of Liverpool Building, Pier Head, 1903–7. [AA035694]*

bulks of machinery, inexhaustible leather and hardware, salt and soap, coals and iron, copper and tin.[2]

But Liverpool was not just a transport hub. It was also a market, where cargoes were bought and sold by merchants and brokers, and where a host of other related businesses flourished, such as banking, insurance and shipowning. It was these trading activities and office-based professions that shaped the centre of Liverpool, making it the earliest fully developed business district in any British city outside London.

The commercial heart of Liverpool described in this book (*see* map p 95) occupies more or less the same site as the original medieval town, established 800 years ago. This was a small settlement on a triangular tongue of land between the Mersey and the Pool (a tidal creek, now filled in, but originally following the line of Whitechapel and Paradise Street). Canning Place, on the site of the Pool mouth, forms the southern tip of the triangle, while Leeds Street may be taken as its northern edge. On this peninsula in the early 13th century a simple arrangement of seven streets was laid out, the pattern of which can still be traced: Old Hall Street, High Street and Castle Street form a central spine, from which Water

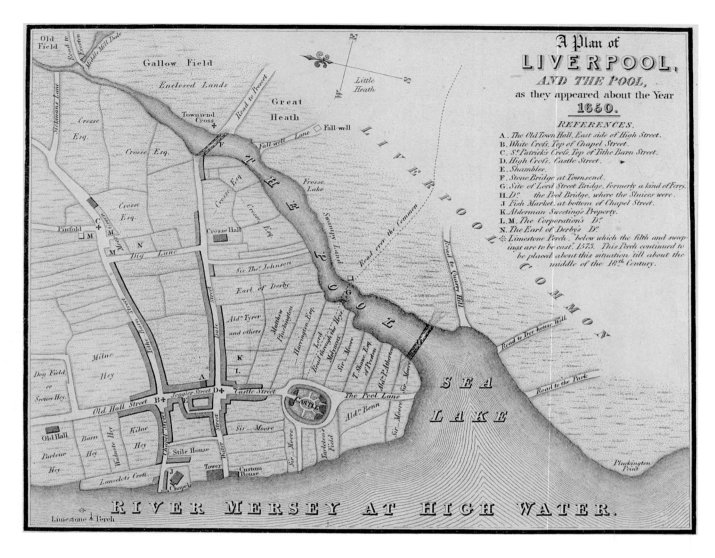

Street and Chapel Street extend westward towards the river while Dale Street and Tithebarn Street lead inland (Fig 5). At high water the Mersey originally followed the line of the Strand, but in the 18th and 19th centuries a wide strip of foreshore was reclaimed from the river for dock construction, and around 1900 one of the earliest docks was built over, creating the Pier Head as an extension of the older business district (Fig 6).

Figure 5 Conjectural plan of Liverpool's seven medieval streets. [From The Stranger in Liverpool, *1829, Liverpool Record Office, Liverpool Libraries]*

Figure 6 *The Pier Head. In the early 20th century Liverpool's commercial architecture reached a climax here in the Port of Liverpool Building, Cunard Building and Royal Liver Building.* [AA017867]

In this area, nothing remains of any medieval building, or indeed of any building earlier than the mid-18th century. A castle stood on the site now occupied by the Queen Victoria monument in Derby Square, and is recalled in the name of Castle Street, but its ruins were cleared away in the 1720s. The fortified tower of the Stanley family stood at the foot of Water Street, but the only trace of it today is in the name of Tower Buildings, an early 20th-century office block that stands in its

Figure 7 *Tower Buildings, Water Street, an office block of 1906–10 designed by Walter Aubrey Thomas. Its turreted roofline evokes the medieval fortified tower of the Stanley family that once stood here.* [AA029296]

place (Fig 7). The church of Our Lady and St Nicholas occupies a venerable site, but no part pre-dates the early 19th century. Indeed, Liverpool is remarkable for the thoroughness with which its early buildings were erased during two centuries of phenomenal growth and prosperity, when historical considerations always took second place to commercial interests. Near the junction of High Street, Dale Street and Castle Street stood the original Town Hall. It was rebuilt in 1673 and raised above an arcaded ground floor, which served the town's merchants as a meeting place and public exchange. This in turn was replaced in 1749–54 with a sumptuous new building on an adjacent site designed by John Wood of Bath (Fig 8). It had a central arcaded court for the merchants, and assembly rooms and a council chamber on the upper floor. The south and east fronts survive, considerably altered, with panels of carving alluding to the slave trade (Fig 9).

The town's narrow medieval boundaries contained it until the end of the 17th century, when the development of land east of the Pool began. A new church – St Peter's – was completed in 1704 in what is now Church

Figure 8 *Liverpool Town Hall. John Wood's building of 1749–54 was gutted by fire in 1795. It was given its present dome in 1802 and its entrance portico in 1811. Originally it had a central open courtyard, intended as an Exchange for the town's merchants. [AA029089]*

Figure 9 *This mid-18th-century sculpture on the Town Hall illustrates the building's commercial role. Elephant tusks, exotic foliage and an African head allude to trade with Africa, including the slave trade. [DP034133]*

Street, and adjoining streets and squares were laid out during the course of the 18th century. More significantly, an enclosed wet dock, the first such for commercial purposes anywhere in the world, was constructed within the mouth of the Pool in 1710–16, on the site now occupied by Canning Place. A Custom House was built beside it, and new streets such as Duke Street and Hanover Street – containing merchants' dwellings, warehouses and counting houses – radiated from it. But although the dock was an important new focus, commercial activity was spread throughout the compact town. The business of an 18th-century merchant was generally conducted from a counting house and warehouse attached to his dwelling, and the appearance of the principal streets was still largely residential. Few houses of this period remain in the area covered by this book, but there is a modest one at 7 Union Street, and a more impressive terrace of three at 135–139 Dale Street, with a grand entrance front in Trueman Street (Fig 10). The Dale Street houses were built *c*1788 by a distiller, John Houghton, whose works adjoined them.

By the middle of the 18th century several coffee houses had opened near the Town Hall, where merchants could meet to discuss business and where public sales were held. It was not until the beginning of the 19th century, however, that the old medieval core began to emerge as the town's dominant business district. The key event was the replacement of the inadequate exchange accommodation in John Wood's Town Hall with the ambitious new Exchange Buildings behind. Erected in 1803–8 to the designs of John Foster Senior, possibly with the assistance of James Wyatt, this U-shaped neoclassical block enclosed three sides of a quadrangle – the Exchange Flags – where merchants transacted business in the open air (Fig 11). There was a newsroom in the east wing (Fig 12),

Figure 10 *139 Dale Street, at the corner of Trueman Street, a house of c1788 built by the distiller John Houghton. [AA037365]*

Figure 11 *The Exchange Flags and the first Exchange Buildings of 1803–8. [19th-century print, Liverpool Record Office, Liverpool Libraries, Hf 942.7213 EXC]*

Figure 12 *Interior of the Exchange newsroom. [19th-century print, Liverpool Record Office, Liverpool Libraries, Hf 942.7213 EXC]*

where subscribers had access to the newspapers that were their chief source of commercial information, and above this was an underwriters' room. The other two wings consisted of offices and warehousing let to merchants. Though its great size and architectural ambition made it seem like a public undertaking for the improvement of the town, it was in fact an entirely commercial effort, paid for by shareholders seeking a return on their investment. Thomas Troughton, writing in 1810, described it as perhaps 'the most splendid structure ever raised, in modern times, for purposes merely commercial'.[3] It was rebuilt on a much enlarged scale in the 1860s (see Fig 45) to a design in French Renaissance style by T H Wyatt, this in turn being replaced in the 1930s to 1950s with the even bigger building by Gunton & Gunton which exists today.

The Exchange, comprising the Exchange Buildings and the Flags, quickly became the focus of the town's economic life. Before the adoption of the telephone (from 1879) face-to-face contact and physical proximity were essential for doing business, and this helped create a highly concentrated business district. Brokers wanted to be able to call personally on many potential customers in quick succession and to have access to the commercial intelligence provided by the newsroom, and clerks needed to hurry between the Flags and their offices, carrying urgent information on behalf of their employers. In the 1850s and 1860s especially, the Exchange became a magnet for speculative office developments and the headquarters of financial institutions. Property prices in its vicinity rose to levels that attracted national attention, and the surrounding streets were almost entirely rebuilt. Newspaper advertisements for offices to let laid great stress on closeness to the Exchange, which was the undisputed centre of business activity (see Fig 53).

Complementary to the emerging business district, other specialised zones developed east of it in the course of the 19th century. Shopping was concentrated around Church Street and cultural provision around St George's Hall, while high-class housing colonised the Mosslake Fields area centred on Abercromby Square, before spreading to more distant suburbs. In 1873 the architect and historian J A Picton, who lived through

Figure 13 *Former Victoria Chapel, Crosshall Street, 1878–80, by W H Picton, son of the architect and historian J A Picton. [AA030921]*

this period of change, described the transformation that had taken place since the beginning of the century: in those early years 'the merchant or broker lived in the town and was of it', but by the 1870s the centre was largely populated by commuting office-workers, and had become 'a sphere to do business in, to make money or – to lose it; but that done, the omnibus, the steamboat, the railway, whirl off their thousands to purer air and brighter skies'.[4]

The loss of a resident population from the city centre is reflected in the disappearance of places of worship. Only the parish church of Our Lady and St Nicholas is still used for its original purpose, and the one other surviving religious building is the former Victoria Chapel in Crosshall Street, a Welsh Calvinistic Methodist building of 1878–80 (Fig 13). Of 18th-century foundations, the Anglican St George's, Derby Square, was demolished in 1897 to make way for the Queen Victoria monument, and St Paul's, St Paul's Square, in 1932. Two Roman Catholic churches – St Mary's, Highfield Street and Holy Cross, Great Crosshall Street – have been demolished since 2000. They were a reminder that just north of the palatial commercial buildings of Dale Street, and particularly north of Tithebarn Street, the Victorian centre changed dramatically and was dominated by dense housing, occupied by a poor and largely Irish population. Charles Goad's insurance plans of 1888 show many very small and confined dwellings in narrow lanes leading off Dale Street (Fig 14), one of which survives in Hockenhall Alley, absorbed into the side of the grandiose Princes Buildings (Fig 15). Goad's plans also show that even at this date processes such as brewing, distilling and foundry work were being carried on within the commercial centre, alongside crowded dwellings and prestigious office blocks. Indeed, Princes Buildings itself was built in 1882 to accommodate leather works for the firm of George Angus & Co, along with offices and shops (Fig 16).

The creation of the new Exchange Buildings and Exchange Flags at the start of the 19th century brought orderliness and open space into the heart of the town, replacing a dense area of irregular buildings. It was part of the gradual transformation of the congested centre begun in 1786, when the Corporation applied successfully to Parliament for an

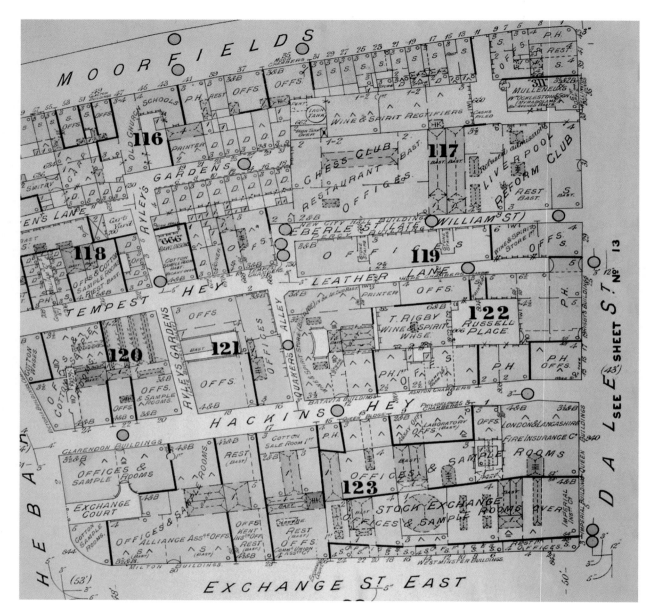

Figure 14 *On Charles Goad's fire insurance plans of 1888, industrial premises and small dwellings, marked 'D', lie just behind the grand commercial buildings of Dale Street. [Liverpool Record Office, Liverpool Libraries]*

Figure 15 *An early 19th-century house in Hockenhall Alley, absorbed into Princes Buildings. [DP28728]*

Figure 16 *Princes Buildings, Dale Street, 1882, by Henry Shelmerdine. [AA042273]*

Figure 17 *The west side of Castle Street being demolished and rebuilt to a new line in 1786. This transformed the narrow medieval street into a dignified thoroughfare, ending with a view of the Town Hall. [Watercolour, Herdman Collection 1267A, Liverpool Record Office, Liverpool Libraries]*

Improvement Act to widen Castle Street (Fig 17). Further acts were obtained during the course of the following century, empowering the Corporation to widen and straighten older streets and make entirely new ones, thus improving communications and sanitary conditions, and creating new opportunities for architectural display. These changes involved the Corporation in complex negotiations over the acquisition of sites, compensation payments to owners, and supervision of the rebuilding process to achieve improved architectural standards. The pattern of rebuilding tended towards the consolidation of sites previously in multiple ownership, so that over time single large buildings replaced numerous smaller ones.

Transport was the reason for Liverpool's very existence. Goods and passengers had to traverse the town on the way to and from the river, and as the docks expanded and traffic increased, the widening of the narrow medieval streets became a commercial necessity. Other means of transport also helped shape the growth of the centre. The Leeds and Liverpool Canal opened in 1774 and had its terminus in Old Hall Street.

Figure 18 *Stained glass in the Railway public house, Tithebarn Street, showing the rebuilt terminus of the Lancashire & Yorkshire Railway. [DP28698]*

It provided passenger transport by boat for merchants living out of town along its route, but it also spawned coal yards and wharfs, which later discouraged the northward expansion of the office district. Much more influential were the railways. The Liverpool terminus of the Lancashire & Yorkshire Railway opened in Tithebarn Street in 1850 and had a marked impact on the pattern of office development. New buildings sprang up beside it, conveniently situated for businessmen visiting Liverpool from the manufacturing towns of east Lancashire and west Yorkshire, and for daily commuters who could afford to live in the salubrious residential areas that developed along the Lancashire coast towards Southport. Renamed Exchange Station, it was completely rebuilt and doubled in size in the 1880s (Fig 18). Only the frontage survives today, incorporated into the Mercury Court office development. In 1886 the under-river Mersey Railway opened, supplementing the ferries from the Pier Head as a means of reaching the Cheshire shore. From its low-level station in James Street, connected by pedestrian tunnel with Water Street, it opened up new dormitory suburbs on the Wirral to commuting clerks and merchants. Finally, in 1893, came the Liverpool Overhead Railway. Running above the dock road, it was the world's first elevated

Figure 19 *George's Dock Ventilation and Control Station, Pier Head, by Herbert J Rowse, 1932, for the first Mersey road tunnel, Queensway. [AA031145]*

electric railway, and eventually extended for 14.5km from the Dingle at the south end to Seaforth at the north. It had stations at the Pier Head and James Street, serving office workers commuting to and from their homes, and travelling between the business district and the various docks.

Horse-drawn omnibuses (from the 1830s) and trams (from 1869) also linked the commercial centre with suburban areas. Early omnibus routes terminated at inns in Dale Street, as had the stagecoaches of the pre-railway era, but in 1882 tram routes were extended to the Pier Head, which became a busy interchange for land and water transport. In the early 20th century the impact of the motor car began to be felt in the city centre. The entrances and ventilating towers of Queensway, the first road tunnel under the Mersey (1925–34), were conceived as major architectural contributions to the business district (Fig 19), and Gunton & Gunton's 1937 designs for replacing the Exchange Buildings incorporated a pioneering underground car park below the Flags.

Though many individual buildings have survived from the city's Victorian and Edwardian heyday, an effort of imagination is now needed to recreate the bustling commercial life that once animated them. Something of its flavour was captured by the former cotton trader John Owen, who in his 1921 novel *The Cotton Broker* recalled the Liverpool he had known before the First World War

the hurrying men, the big sleek horses, the lorries loaded house-high with bales of cotton, or crates of fruit or chests of tea; the crowded streets with perspiring policemen waving arms to keep open the long lines of traffic; the great offices, that each year seemed to rise higher, and every window in which looked like one of the myriad eyes of this great monster of Trade.[5]

CHAPTER 2

Specialised zones

Between our produce and provision men, our cotton and corn brokers, our general merchants and our great shipping houses, I rather suspect we pretty well run creation.

Liverpool Review, 1886[6]

In 19th-century Liverpool, related business activities tended to concentrate in well-defined areas, so the commercial centre comprised a number of lesser centres, each with its own specialised resources.

The Exchange was the principal hub and served also as the focus of the all-important cotton trade during most of the 19th century: when the diarist Francis Kilvert visited in 1872, he noted that the Flags were white with scraps of cotton wool discarded by the merchants. The surrounding streets were densely packed with the offices of cotton traders, and sample rooms, where the quality of different lots of raw cotton could be compared. Surviving examples include Mason's Building in Exchange Street East (Fig 20), the Albany Building in Old Hall Street (*see* Figs 36, 84 and 85) and Berey's Buildings in Bixteth Street (Fig 21). In 1896 the cotton trade moved indoors from the Flags to converted premises in neighbouring Brown's Buildings (on the site now occupied by Martins Bank Building), and from there to the spectacular new Cotton Exchange in Old Hall Street, opened 10 years later (*see* Fig 65). Its stupendous baroque façade has been demolished, but the enormous scale of what remains bears witness to the dominance of King Cotton.

The first purpose-built Corn Exchange opened in Brunswick Street in 1808, in a building designed by John Foster Senior. It was rebuilt in 1853–4 by J A Picton, and again in 1953–9 following destruction in the Second World War. Corn merchants' offices gravitated to the surrounding area, but most have now been demolished. The specialist trade best represented by surviving 19th-century buildings is that in fruit and produce (including cured meats, tinned fish, butter and cheese), which was concentrated in and around Victoria Street. The creation of this new street in the 1860s coincided exactly with the rapid expansion of the produce trade, brought about by fast, reliable steamships and by the spread of the American railway system. The burgeoning output of the United States flowed into Victoria Street, where the first building erected

Figure 20 *Mason's Building, Exchange Street East, c1866, by John Cunningham. [AA029117]*

Figure 21 *Berey's Buildings, corner of Bixteth Street and George Street, a speculative office block of 1864. The drawings are signed by William Culshaw, but the design was probably made by his future partner Henry Sumners. [AA030891]*

Figure 22 *Fowler's Buildings, Victoria Street, 1865–9,*
by J A Picton. [AA029068]

was Fowler's Buildings for the American produce importers Fowler Brothers (Fig 22). A Produce Newsroom was established nearby in Victoria Buildings in 1886, and Produce Exchange Buildings opened on the opposite side of the street in 1902 (Fig 23). Meanwhile, leading fruit merchants built the Commercial Saleroom Buildings at the corner of

Figure 23 *Produce Exchange Buildings, Victoria Street, 1902, by Henry Shelmerdine. The ground floor was originally a goods depot for the Lancashire & Yorkshire Railway. On the left is part of the Fruit Exchange, converted from a goods depot of the London & North Western Railway. [AA029110]*

Victoria Street and Temple Court in 1879, for conducting wholesale auctions of imported fruit (Fig 24), and when the trade outgrew this accommodation it was supplemented in 1924 by a new Fruit Exchange next door, converted from a former goods depot of the London & North Western Railway.

Lawyers and accountants were essential to the operation of the business district and many were to be found around Cook Street, Harrington Street and North and South John streets. Some had the professional expertise (and access to the necessary financial resources) to act as property developers, and they occupied offices in buildings they had raised themselves. The block at the corner of Cook Street and North

Figure 24 *Commercial Saleroom Buildings, corner of Victoria Street and Temple Court, 1879, by James F Doyle. In the mid-1880s, the busy ground-floor saleroom dealt with an average of 30,000 barrels of North American apples a week. [AA040558]*

Figure 25 *27 Castle Street, 1846. Offices with ground-floor shops, designed for Ambrose Lace probably by A H Holme. [AA029225]*

John Street was built by the lawyer Thomas Avison, whose initials appear on a rainwater head with the date 1828. It was apparently designed by John Foster Junior. Harrington Chambers (*see* Fig 35), next door, was developed around 1830 by the accountant Harmood Banner, while the attorney Ambrose Lace built unusually distinguished premises for himself at 27 Castle Street in 1846 (Fig 25). A focus for the legal profession was the Law Association building in Cook Street. Now demolished, the former entrance to its library survives at number 14.

Castle Street and its tributaries became Liverpool's unrivalled centre for financial services during the course of the 19th century. As early as the 1770s the private bank of Messrs Heywood occupied premises in Castle Street, before moving round the corner to Brunswick Street in about 1800. Its new, purpose-built home was the first showpiece financial building in the area (Fig 26), but other banks at this date were

Figure 26 *Heywood's Bank, Brunswick Street, 1798–1800. The bank included living accommodation: a house is attached in Fenwick Street, visible on the right. [AA029139]*

widely scattered, and when the Bank of England was seeking premises for its first Liverpool branch in 1826, it settled on a former private house in Hanover Street, close to the Custom House. The setting up of joint-stock banks in provincial towns was permitted from 1826, and in the late 1830s three such banks built premises close to Castle Street: the North & South Wales Bank in Derby Square (Fig 27), the Union Bank in Brunswick Street, and the Royal Bank just off Dale Street (Fig 28). In 1844 the Bank of England itself bought a site at the corner of Castle and Cook streets for its monumental new building (*see* Fig 41) and the Commercial Bank rose on the neighbouring corner at exactly the same

Figure 27 *North & South Wales Bank, Derby Square, 1838–40, by Edward Corbett. [AA040501]*

Figure 28 *Royal Bank, Queen Avenue, Dale Street, c1837–8, by Samuel Rowland. Later it housed the Queen Insurance Co. [AA029097]*

time. Thereafter virtually all new head offices of banks were built in or very near to Castle Street, which became one of the most opulent Victorian commercial streets in the country.

Insurance offices also clustered in Castle Street and at the west end of Dale Street, where the Royal Insurance Co built its first head office at the corner of North John Street in 1848 (replaced 1896–1903). In the 1850s the Liverpool & London Insurance Co erected palatial headquarters at 1 Dale Street (*see* Fig 40) and the Queen Insurance Co followed suit at number 11 (*see* Fig 38). In Castle Street in the 1870s

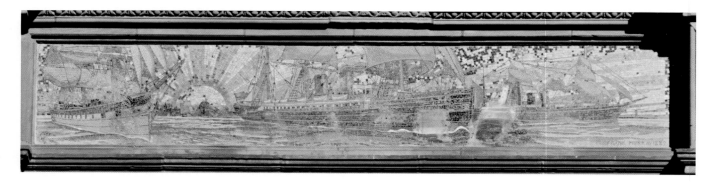

and 1880s, the architects G E Grayson and E A Ould rebuilt numbers 3–25 – almost an entire block – with insurance and life assurance offices, including the British & Foreign Marine with its colourful mosaic frieze depicting shipping (Fig 29). The greatest insurance headquarters of all, the Royal Liver Building (*see* Fig 73), stands apart from this group in splendid isolation at the Pier Head. The Royal Liver Friendly Society moved there in 1911, from more modest premises outside the commercial centre.

Shipping companies, as might be expected, clustered near the river, the main concentrations being in and around Water Street and James Street. The majority occupied premises in speculative office blocks such as Tower Buildings and India Buildings, both in Water Street. By contrast, the mighty, turreted White Star Line building in James Street and the magnificent Cunard Building at the Pier Head (Figs 30 and 31) advertised the special status of the companies whose names they bore.

Although dominated by commerce, Liverpool's business district was also the centre of local government. The Town Hall housed most of the Corporation's offices until 1867–8, when the palatial new Municipal Buildings at the other end of Dale Street opened (Fig 32). This giant office block joined the 1857–9 Magistrates' Courts, Bridewell and Fire Station (the latter rebuilt in 1895–8), and was followed by the Education Offices of 1897–8 in Sir Thomas Street and the Tramway Offices of 1905–7 in Hatton Garden, creating a well-defined precinct for municipal

Figure 29 *Detail of mosaic frieze, designed by Frank Murray and made by Salviati for the British & Foreign Marine Insurance Co, Castle Street, 1889. [AA029354]*

Figure 30 (above, left) *White Star Line building, James Street, 1895–8, by Richard Norman Shaw. The gable was simplified when it was rebuilt after wartime bomb damage. [AA040458]*

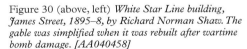

Figure 31 (above, right) *Cunard Building, by Willink & Thicknesse with Arthur J Davis, 1914–16. [AA017862]*

administration. Its proximity to the area round the Exchange had practical advantages: members of the Council were drawn from the town's business elite, and had to move regularly between the sphere of local government and the offices where they carried on their professions.

Somewhat removed from the centre of commercial and municipal activity is Canning Place, where in the 1820s the Old Dock was filled in and a colossal new Custom House built to the designs of John Foster Junior. It housed the Government's revenue offices and the General Post Office, and until the construction of the new Mersey Docks and Harbour Board offices at the Pier Head in 1903–7 it was also the administrative

Figure 32 *Left, the Municipal Buildings, Dale Street, 1862–8, by John Weightman and E R Robson, and right, the former Conservative Club, 1880–3, by F & G Holme. [AA029373]*

centre for the port. Its remoteness was considered a disadvantage, and some of its functions were later transferred to new accommodation in Victoria Street. Government Buildings, a large and dignified block housing the Inland Revenue and other offices, was erected directly behind the Municipal Buildings in about 1880 (it was demolished following wartime bomb damage), and on the opposite side of the street a new and exceptionally large General Post Office was built in 1894–9. Part of its façade survives, incorporated into the Met Quarter shopping centre.

CHAPTER 3

Office buildings

In Liverpool there appears to be a passion for building blocks of offices under one roof, with a club-house aspect.

The Builder, 1858[7]

Origin and development

Purpose-designed offices have been the defining building type of central Liverpool since the middle of the 19th century, but their origins can be traced back to the late 18th century. In 1786 the Corporation cleared an area of older buildings just west of the Town Hall, and on part of the site erected Exchange Alley, a speculative development of offices for rent to brokers. Exchange Alley was a narrow courtyard, entered through an archway at one end, with ranges of two-storey buildings on each side (Fig 33). These contained offices fitted up by the Corporation to suit the needs of tenants, including several cotton traders. The Corporation evidently thought the office rental market was likely to grow and was anxious to protect its investment. It ordered that in all conveyances of Corporation property nearby, a covenant should be inserted 'on the part of purchasers not to let or suffer to be occupied any part of their buildings as brokers' offices for the space of three years'.[8] The new Exchange of 1803–8 was, as we have seen, largely a speculative development of merchants' offices and warehouses, built by a company specially formed for the purpose. It must have stimulated smaller property owners to follow suit, for in 1805 James Hargraves, a hatter, erected Hargraves Buildings on the east side of the Town Hall, carrying on his business in part and letting the rest as offices. It would be surprising if this was an isolated case.

An Improvement Act obtained by the Corporation in 1826 gave a further boost to office building. Under it, the Corporation Surveyor John Foster Junior oversaw the creation of St George's Crescent and the widening of Lord Street and North and South John streets (Fig 34). These were largely rebuilt again during the course of the late 19th and 20th centuries, but on the west side of North John Street some of the original buildings of the 1820s to 1840s survive (Fig 35). They are four-storey stuccoed blocks with Classical details,

The distinctive projecting windows of Oriel Chambers in Water Street, 1864, by Peter Ellis. [AA030741]

taller than the houses they replaced, and very similar to the contemporary commercial street architecture of London. They have – and probably always had – shopfronts on the ground floor, but trade directories show that they were largely occupied as offices by merchants, attorneys and accountants.

A landmark in the development of the speculative office block was the original India Buildings of 1833–4, at the corner of Water Street and Fenwick Street. Built by the merchant George Holt and designed by Joseph Franklin, it was the first really large speculative office building in Liverpool to be erected by a private individual. Holt had planned a mixture of offices and warehouses on the site – it was standard practice to combine the two functions – but changed his mind on realizing the greater profitability of offices. Arranged round a central court, India Buildings varied between three and four storeys, and contained accommodation for over 60 businesses. The offices were reached from eight spacious, top-lit staircases, and WCs were provided on the landings and elsewhere (*see* Fig 49c). So successful was the development that Holt added further blocks in the 1840s, extending southward as far as Brunswick Street. The whole complex was only demolished in the 1920s when the site was required for the present India Buildings (*see* Fig 75), which covered more than twice the area of its predecessor.

Importantly for Liverpool's future development, Holt's business acumen was combined with a sense of civic duty. He wanted his new office block to be an ornament to the town – 'most substantial & handsome … capable of standing perhaps for hundreds of years'[9] – so he gave it imposing Classical façades of stucco and stone, with giant Ionic pilasters to the upper floors. His example was followed by other speculators – merchants, bankers and financial institutions – who recognized the profits to be made from erecting office buildings for the rental market in Liverpool's expanding commercial environment. Between them, they completely transformed the central business streets in the middle decades of the 19th century, replacing utilitarian warehouses and modest domestic buildings of brick with richly decorated Classical office blocks, largely faced in stone. *Whitty's Guide to Liverpool* of 1871 described the rapid process of transformation

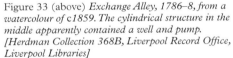

Figure 33 (above) *Exchange Alley, 1786–8, from a watercolour of c1859. The cylindrical structure in the middle apparently contained a well and pump. [Herdman Collection 368B, Liverpool Record Office, Liverpool Libraries]*

Figure 34 (above, right) *This 1836 map shows North and South John Streets and Lord Street after widening in the 1820s. Dale Street and Water Street had only been widened in parts at this date, but the process continued through the 19th century. [From M A Gage's* Trigonometrical plan of the town and port of Liverpool, *1836, Liverpool Record Office, Liverpool Libraries]*

Figure 35 (right) *Harrington Chambers, North John Street: shops and offices of c1830. [AA040900]*

Figure 36 *Albany Building, Old Hall Street. This exceptionally large speculative office block of 1856–8 was designed by J K Colling for the banker R C Naylor. [AA030889]*

In no other particular has Liverpool more advanced than in the improvement of her commercial and mercantile places of business. Within the period of 25 years the offices and counting-houses were for the most part dark, damp, dismal, inconvenient and badly-ventilated places, situated in all sort of out-of-the-way and incommodious localities. They are now the very reverse of this.[10]

From the early 1840s onwards, Liverpool office blocks began to imitate the type of grand, urban, residential building of the Italian Renaissance known as a *palazzo* (palace). The first such was probably Brunswick Buildings, now demolished, at the corner of Brunswick and Fenwick streets, a speculative development designed by A & G Williams for the merchant J C Ewart. It was followed by many more, including such surviving examples as the Albany Building in Old Hall Street (Fig 36), and Hargreaves Buildings in Chapel Street (Fig 37), built by

Figure 37 (above, left) *Hargreaves Buildings, Chapel Street, 1859, by J A Picton. [AA029382]*

Figure 38 (above, right) *11 Dale Street, 1859, designed by J A Picton for the Queen Insurance Co, with speculative offices on the upper floors. [AA029170]*

the bankers R C Naylor and William Brown respectively. The trading cities of Renaissance Italy had an obvious symbolic appeal for Liverpool's merchant princes, and Venice in particular, the seat of a great maritime empire, provided attractive models. The panels of polished granite that decorate 11 Dale Street (Fig 38) are clearly derived from the palaces of the Grand Canal, and the architectural press regularly described Liverpool office blocks as Venetian or 'Venetianised'. Hargreaves Buildings and 11 Dale Street, both designed by J A Picton, include some

Gothic Revival features, but contemporaries were struck by Liverpool's general preference for Classicism, and when the competition for the new Exchange was held in 1863, only three of the 44 designs submitted were Gothic. Picton, writing in 1864, recognized the appropriate symbolism of the *palazzo* style, praising the new office buildings as 'the visible embodiment of modern commerce', and declaring that 'they worthily

Figure 39 *Royal Bank Buildings, designed by Samuel Rowland and built c1837–8. It was set back to a new building line as part of the widening of Dale Street. It was later taken over by the Queen Insurance Co. [AA029307]*

Figure 40 *1 Dale Street, originally the headquarters of the Liverpool & London Insurance Co, 1856–8, by C R Cockerell. It forms a unit with three other office blocks behind, built speculatively by the Company and occupying an extremely valuable site beside the Exchange Flags. The mansard roof was added in the 1920s. [AA040746]*

represent the vast commercial transactions which daily take place within their walls'.[11]

Alongside the growth of speculative office blocks ran the development of prestigious flagship buildings for single firms such as banks and insurance companies. The use of decorative historical styles and costly materials was a form of advertising, allowing them to proclaim their financial standing and respectability (though such conspicuous expenditure also carried the risk of appearing profligate or reckless). To exploit their valuable sites to the full, these firms would generally include a good deal of lettable space along with their own accommodation. This resulted in bigger buildings that announced their status even more loudly, as well as providing space for possible future expansion. When the Royal Bank built its new premises in 1836–9, it developed the larger part of the site fronting Dale Street with a sumptuously decorated speculative office block, Royal Bank Buildings (Fig 39), while the bank itself occupied a smaller detached building at the end of the inner court (*see* Fig 28). Directly opposite, the Liverpool & London Insurance Co employed C R Cockerell in the 1850s to design four *palazzo*-style buildings grouped round a courtyard, forming a single block almost as big as the neighbouring Town Hall (Fig 40). The company only occupied the more elaborate front building, the rest being let to tenants, but its commercial importance was reflected in the grandeur of the whole complex.

Perhaps the most distinguished example of architecture used to assert the status of a financial institution and inspire confidence among its clients is Cockerell's Bank of England in Castle Street, where the giant Doric columns of the façade instil both a sense of awe and a firm belief in the Bank's unshakeable strength and stability (Fig 41). Combining massive bulk with exquisitely refined details, it is one of the masterpieces of Victorian commercial architecture. It contained no lettable space, but the Bank cashed in on the speculative office boom by commissioning Cockerell to design a separate block of offices for rent, next door in Cook Street (it was demolished in 1959).

Figure 41 *The Bank of England's Liverpool branch, 1846–8, by C R Cockerell. The Bank's agent lived at the front of the building overlooking Castle Street, in an apartment entered from Union Court, while the sub-agent lived at the opposite end. The banking hall was in the middle. [AA040554]*

Form and function

Figure 42 *Wrought-iron gate at Commercial Saleroom Buildings, corner of Victoria Street and Temple Court. [DP28858]*

The typical Liverpool office building of the mid-19th century had three principal storeys, plus a semi-basement and attic. Before the introduction of lifts (gradually from the 1860s, but more widely from the 1880s) it was uneconomical to build any higher, since the upper floors would be difficult to let. The well-lit semi-basement, on the other hand, reached by a short flight of steps from pavement level, was as readily accessible as the ground floor, and was often occupied by offices; shops and other traders were also accommodated here. A list of tenants' names was displayed beside the entrance, or painted directly on the wall. Steps led up from pavement to ground floor, from where one or more staircases rose through the height of the building. To help ventilate stairs and corridors, the street entrance was often closed with an iron gate rather than a solid door: there are surviving examples at the Albany, at Central Buildings in North John Street, and at several buildings in Victoria Street (Fig 42). Washbasins were often provided within each office suite, but toilets were almost always in the attic, the part of the building that commanded the lowest rents. (Until the First World War men were overwhelmingly dominant in the office workplace: the Cotton Exchange, opened in 1906, was equipped with 64 male WCs and numerous urinals, but only 7 female WCs.) A flat was usually also provided in the attic for the caretaker and his family. There was often a windowless sub-basement which could be let as bonded warehousing, so the owner of the building could derive as much income as possible from his expensively acquired site. Cast-iron hoists – for instance in Sweeting Street and Hackins Hey (Fig 43) – survive as evidence of such underground storage. In general, such bonded vaults were probably not used by the merchants who occupied the offices above.

In the all-important cotton trade, an early 19th-century merchant's office was generally combined with warehousing on the upper floors, allowing potential buyers to inspect the bales of raw cotton thoroughly before making a purchase. Over time, however, improvements in the sorting and packing of raw cotton by American growers meant that bales became more consistent in quality and volume, which in turn meant that dealers and spinners could decide whether to purchase by examining a small sample of cotton, without having to inspect each bale individually. The result was that by the 1850s office and warehouse became separated. The goods in which a merchant dealt would be stored in the growing ranks of warehouses close to the docks, while meetings, paperwork, and the inspection of samples would be conducted at an office in the business district. At the same time, rapidly rising land values in the vicinity of the Exchange were a strong inducement to build office blocks in place of warehouses. The clearest illustration of this trend is the decision to rebuild Exchange Buildings itself in the 1860s. Most of the old 1803–8 Exchange Buildings consisted of ground-floor offices with warehousing above, which by the 1860s was a very unprofitable use for an extremely valuable site; the proprietors therefore decided to demolish it and erect a new building consisting of offices and salerooms only (Figs 44 and 45). One supporter of rebuilding was the merchant banker William Brown, who had invested heavily in speculative office building on his own

Figure 43 (above) *An unusually decorative cast-iron hoist in Hackins Hey, originally serving the basement of 11 Dale Street. [Joseph Sharples]*

Figure 44 (left) *This unique photograph of c1864 shows the commercial centre at a time of dramatic transformation. On the right, the 1803–8 Exchange Buildings are in the course of demolition. To the left are the newly completed Brown's Buildings (on the site now occupied by Martins Bank Building) while behind is a row of warehouses in Rumford Street, soon afterwards replaced with offices. [NMR 96784]*

Figure 45 *The second Exchange Buildings by T H Wyatt, begun in 1864. [19th-century print, Liverpool Record Office, Liverpool Libraries, Hf 942.7213 EXC]*

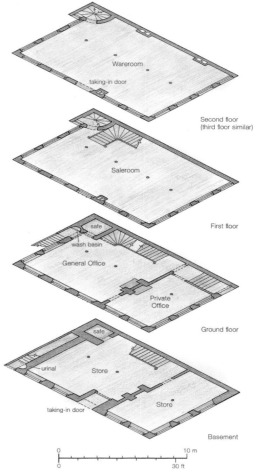

account, and who said that offices such as Hargreaves Buildings (*see* Fig 37) earned him almost twice the revenue of the old office-warehouse buildings they replaced. A combined office and warehouse designed in 1849 for the brokers Rowlinson, Sons & Co survives in Tempest Hey (Figs 46 and 47), but it was probably old-fashioned for its date.

In one important branch of Liverpool commerce, the fruit and provision trade, office accommodation and storage continued under the same roof. For merchants dealing in relatively small quantities of perishable goods, not too bulky and with a fairly rapid turnover, this

Figure 46 (above, left) *Premises in Tempest Hey designed by William Culshaw in 1849 for the brokers Rowlinson, Sons & Co. [DP28723]*

Figure 47 (above, right) *Internal arrangement of Messrs Rowlinson's premises. [Based, with the consent of Edmund Kirby & Sons, on William Culshaw's drawings, Lancashire Record Office, DDX 162, 23/49–53]*

Figure 48 *Granite Buildings, Stanley Street,* c1882, *by G E Grayson. The imposing office façade contrasts with a utilitarian warehouse elevation to the rear.* [DP054462]

seems to have been the preferred arrangement. In Victoria Street and Stanley Street numerous blocks survive from the 1860s to the 1880s, built to accommodate offices and wholesale warehousing for dealers in cheese, bacon, butter and fresh and dried fruit. An outstanding example is Granite Buildings of c1882, by G E Grayson. It has an imposing pedimented façade to Stanley Street (Fig 48) from which its several suites of offices were entered, but much of the rear elevation to Progress Place is treated as a series of gabled warehouses with vertical rows of taking-in doors. Originally a gas engine drove shafting that extended the

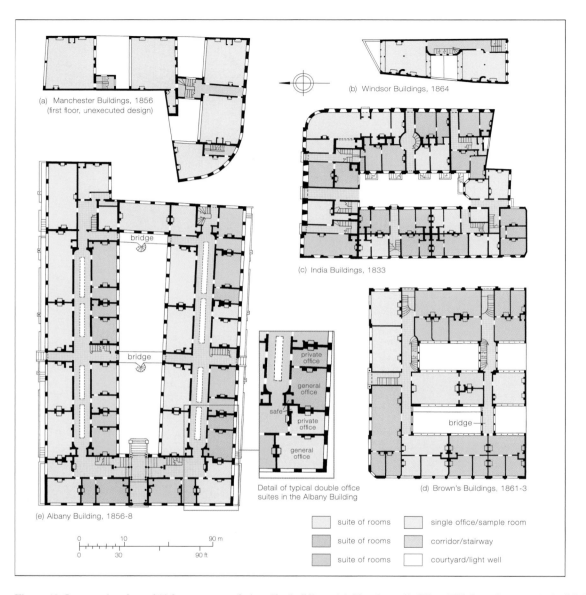

(a) Manchester Buildings, 1856
(first floor, unexecuted design)

(b) Windsor Buildings, 1864

(c) India Buildings, 1833

bridge

bridge

Detail of typical double office
suites in the Albany Building

private
office

general
office

safe

private
office

general
office

bridge

(d) Brown's Buildings, 1861-3

(e) Albany Building, 1856-8

suite of rooms	single office/sample room
suite of rooms	corridor/stairway
suite of rooms	courtyard/light well

0   10   90 m
0   30   90 ft

Figure 49 *Comparative plans of 19th-century speculative office buildings: (a) Manchester Buildings, Tithebarn Street, 1856, by J D Jee for Thomas Joynson; demolished; redrawn from a plan in Liverpool Record Office, Liverpool Libraries, Acc. 2961; (b) Windsor Buildings, George Street, 1864, by William Culshaw for William Higgins; redrawn with the consent of Edmund Kirby & Sons from plans in the Lancashire Record Office, DDX 162, 29/11–12, and 35–39; (c) the original India Buildings, Water Street, 1833–4, by Joseph Franklin for George Holt; demolished; redrawn from plans in Liverpool Record Office, Liverpool Libraries, Hf 942.7213 IND; (d) Brown's Buildings, on the site now occupied by Martins Bank Building, 1861–3, by J A Picton for Sir William Brown; demolished; redrawn from a plan in* The Builder, *16 March 1861; (e) Albany Building, Old Hall Street, 1856–8, by J K Colling for R C Naylor; redrawn from the architect's signed plan in the possession of the Naylor Trust.*

length of the building, raising and lowering merchandise throughout the block. Neighbouring buildings with no rear access have taking-in doors that open directly onto Stanley Street, so their warehousing role is more obvious.

Office plans did not vary greatly in essentials (Figs 49a–e). The simplest might consist of a single room. A common arrangement was the 'double office' comprising two interconnected rooms, an outer general office for the clerks and an inner private room for the proprietor or partners (Fig 50). Usually there would also be a strong room or walk-in safe, sometimes called a book case (Fig 51). It had thick walls and an iron door, and was used for the secure storage of ledgers. Larger businesses might occupy more rooms, or an entire floor of the building. The private office would be furnished with a desk – perhaps a double-sided one where two partners sat face to face – and additional chairs for visitors. The general office would have long sloping desks at which clerks sat on high stools, and in larger establishments there would be partitioned-off spaces for more senior staff. There would often be an area accessible to the public, separated from the clerks by a counter where clients could make or receive payments. These general arrangements lasted well into the 20th century (Fig 52). There might also be sample rooms, where goods for sale could be examined in strong light. Cotton sample rooms in particular needed abundant light for examining cotton wool fibres, and were therefore provided with very large windows directly over the counters. Northern light was preferred, being more even and varying less in the course of the day, and advertisements for offices to let would make a point of saying if the accommodation was north-facing and had good 'cotton lights' (Fig 53).

In the early 19th century, office interiors were generally rather rough and ready in appearance. H E Stripe, who worked in the 1830s and 1840s in the office of Messrs Bibby, iron merchants, recalled it as being 'meanly fitted up – no mahogany to be seen anywhere – only a slight wooden partition separating the private from general office – a similar partition to the manager's office – none of the desks were worth looking at – no uniformity in chairs or stools – the cash keeper in a small cramped up space without room to move'; and he believed this was 'only a fair

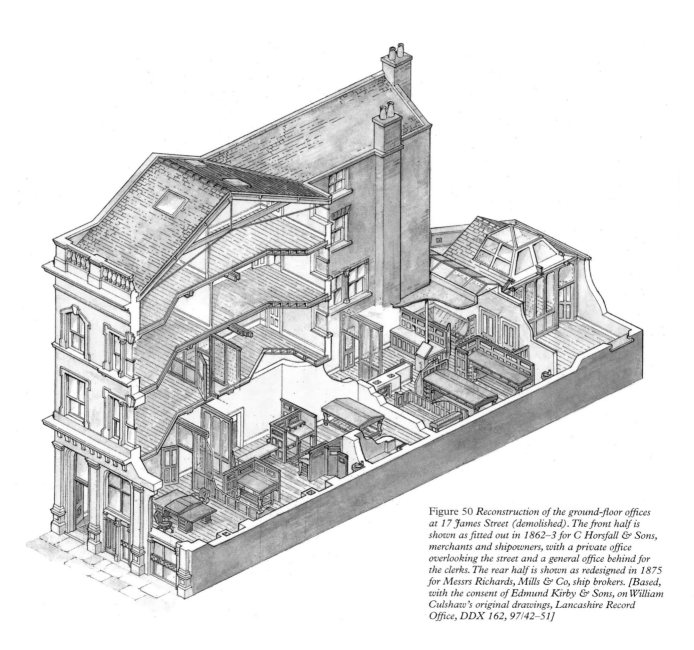

Figure 50 *Reconstruction of the ground-floor offices at 17 James Street (demolished). The front half is shown as fitted out in 1862–3 for C Horsfall & Sons, merchants and shipowners, with a private office overlooking the street and a general office behind for the clerks. The rear half is shown as redesigned in 1875 for Messrs Richards, Mills & Co, ship brokers. [Based, with the consent of Edmund Kirby & Sons, on William Culshaw's original drawings, Lancashire Record Office, DDX 162, 97/42–51]*

Figure 51 (above) *Cast-iron door of a former safe or book case in Harrington Chambers, North John Street, now used as a stockroom by the current occupier, a men's outfitter. [DP28707]*

Figure 52 (above, right) *Interior of the offices of Barber & Garratt, fertiliser importers, Exchange Buildings, 1930s. [Liverpool Record Office, Liverpool Libraries, Acc.4647, box 2]*

Figure 53 (right) *Classified advertisements for offices to let,* Liverpool Mercury, *15 November 1871. [Liverpool Record Office, Liverpool Libraries]*

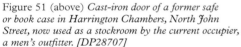

TO BROKERS and Others.—To be Let, the OFFICE, at present and for four years past in the occupation of Messrs. Prowse and Co., in Dod's-buildings, Chapel-street, opposite the Exchange and Newsroom; excellent north light — Apply to the keeper, from ten to eleven in the morning.   15no21

OFFICES to be Let, in the new buildings, Irwell-chambers, Fazakerley-street and Union-street (entrances from both), one minute from the Exchange. Excellent light, lofty and convenient; part have north aspect. Moderate rents.—Apply to Mr. Coates, 14, North John-street.   7node4

OFFICES, with Warehouse, to be Let, in Tempest-hey, communicating with the Exchange, four floors having cotton lights. Suitable for cotton brokers, printers and whole-sale stationers, flannel and woollen warehousemen, dining rooms, &c.—Apply to S. B. Jackson, Swift's-court, 11, Castle-street.   14no20

sample of Merchants' offices in that day'.[12] The cotton broker Thomas Ellison recalled that in the mid-19th century, 'anything in the shape of ornamentation, or in the least degree artistic, raised grave doubts as to the business qualifications of those who indulged in such fripperies'.[13] However, as the century progressed, more attention was given to comfort and style. Businessmen such as the corn merchants Cornelius & Bourgeoise filled their premises with fine furniture and pictures; James Lord Bowes, wool broker and collector of Japanese art, was said to have decorated his office with William Morris wallpaper; and in 1868 the satirical magazine *The Porcupine* noted that 'offices are [now] designed by high-art architects at high-art prices, and are furnished by high-art upholsterers and cabinet-makers in a style of "princely magnificence"'.[14]

Figure 54 (above, left) *Interior of the banking hall, Martins Bank Building, Water Street, 1927–32, by Herbert J Rowse. [Photograph by Stewart Bale, 1932, courtesy of National Museums Liverpool, Merseyside Maritime Museum]*

Figure 55 (above, right) *Shop-lined arcade through the middle of India Buildings, Water Street, 1923–30, by Arnold Thornely and Herbert J Rowse. [FF 000761]*

Figure 56 *Imperial Chambers, Dale Street, c1872. The office windows look onto a central space which rises through the full height of the building to a glass roof. [DP034130]*

Little evidence of such interiors has survived, though the marble-lined lobbies of Commercial Saleroom Buildings and Union House hint at a taste for greater display in the last quarter of the 19th century. Naturally, the public offices of banks and insurance companies were almost always richly appointed. The interiors of the former Royal Bank (1837–8) and Alliance Bank (1868) are relatively early examples of a taste for lavish decoration that culminated in Martins Bank (1927–32), a glorious temple of commerce with travertine columns and gilded ceilings, rich with sculpture and bronze fittings (Fig 54). The circulation spaces of other large office buildings of the early 20th century, such as India Buildings (Fig 55) and the Cunard Building, are similarly palatial.

Lighting and technology

The need for good natural light had a crucial influence on the design of 19th-century offices. Artificial light provided by candles and gas had obvious disadvantages, and even after the introduction of electricity from the late 1870s (and more widely from the 1890s), daylight was still an important requirement. Offices such as Rumford Court and Royal Bank Buildings are grouped around courtyards, an arrangement that provides some seclusion from the noise of the street, but also serves to admit light. At the much larger Albany, the spacious central court is treated as a formal architectural space, with elevations as regular as those facing the street, as in an Italian *palazzo*. Often such courts were roofed with glass and iron and used as circulation spaces, a good surviving example being Imperial Chambers, Dale Street (Fig 56). Many sites, however, were irregular in shape, narrow in proportion to their depth from front to back, and hemmed in by adjoining tall buildings, and in these cases it took considerable ingenuity to devise a plan that would let in plenty of light. As *The Porcupine* noted in 1868

> In not a few instances the architects have had many and serious difficulties to contend with in adopting [sic] the structure to the locality in which it is placed, so as to secure an economical occupation of the

land – generally of very great value – and at the same time to obtain an advantageous distribution of light suited to the display of samples of produce, by means of which a large portion of the commercial business of the community is carried on.[15]

Architects met these challenges by arranging their offices around light wells, which could be made more effective by facing them with reflective white glazed tiles or light-coloured brick. The same materials were widely used in dark, narrow side streets, to reflect light into adjoining buildings (Fig 57).

The size and arrangement of windows offered another way of tackling the problem of natural lighting, but for much of the 19th century architectural tradition in this regard was at odds with more practical considerations. As *The Builder* observed, reviewing the new Exchange Buildings in 1870: 'the problem how to make an architecturally successful building, and yet give the amount of light which cotton salesmen seem to expect, is a task almost beyond the ingenuity of any architect.'[16] Architects were often more obedient to tradition in the main façades of buildings, and more experimental elsewhere. On the entrance front of J A Picton's Hargreaves Buildings (*see* Fig 37), the north-facing windows are derived – like the whole elevation – from an Italian *palazzo*: small in relation to the expanse of solid wall, they are set deep within projecting stone surrounds, further reducing the amount of light they admit. On the less conspicuous side elevation to Covent Garden, however, Picton felt able to introduce bigger windows on the ground and first floors, and bring them closer to the wall surface in a quite unhistorical way. At Windsor Buildings in George Street there was an even greater contrast between the windows of the Renaissance-style façade and those (now demolished) which faced onto the inner courtyard and parallel Edmund Street (Fig 58). J K Colling's Albany also follows the Italian *palazzo* model, but has windows of broader proportions both to the front (*see* Fig 36) and at the sides. Pekin Buildings (*c*1859), in Harrington Street, shows a more radical approach, with paired sash windows producing a façade that is more glass than wall, though still crowned with a big *palazzo*-style cornice (Fig 59).

Figure 57 *Queen Arcade, offices of the 1880s, faced with glazed brick to reflect daylight. [AA029096]*

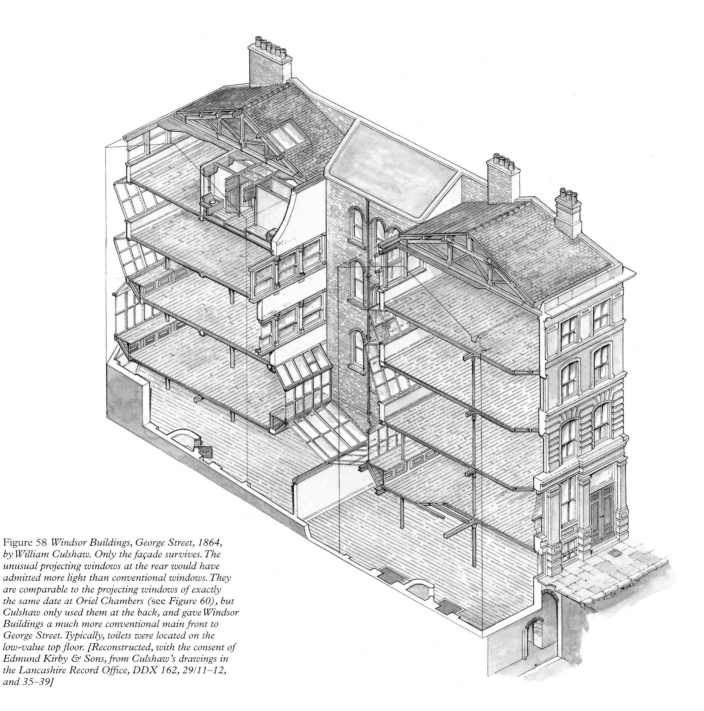

Figure 58 *Windsor Buildings, George Street, 1864, by William Culshaw. Only the façade survives. The unusual projecting windows at the rear would have admitted more light than conventional windows. They are comparable to the projecting windows of exactly the same date at Oriel Chambers (see Figure 60), but Culshaw only used them at the back, and gave Windsor Buildings a much more conventional main front to George Street. Typically, toilets were located on the low-value top floor. [Reconstructed, with the consent of Edmund Kirby & Sons, from Culshaw's drawings in the Lancashire Record Office, DDX 162, 29/11–12, and 35–39]*

The most extreme solution to the lighting problem is represented by the unique Oriel Chambers, Water Street, a sort of Jacobean-cum-Gothic building designed by Peter Ellis and completed in 1864 (Fig 60 and *see* detail on p32). Here the windows actually project from the façade like facetted glass bubbles, separated by the narrowest strips of masonry. Desks positioned within these windows receive light from above and either side, as well as in front, while in the courtyard behind, glass flows continuously along the façade in front of the cast-iron stanchions that support the floors, an early instance of curtain glazing (Fig 61). Projecting windows with sloping glazed tops were not invented by Ellis – an example facing onto the courtyard of an office in Chapel Street, now demolished, was designed by William Culshaw as early as 1846 – but Ellis was exceptional in applying this functional design solution to the main façade of a building, and doing so in one of Liverpool's most prestigious commercial streets. Oriel Chambers was widely condemned in its day as ugly and eccentric, and the experiment was not repeated, though Ellis did design the equally unconventional 16 Cook Street, with a five-storey façade like one giant window, and more curtain-glazing at the rear (Fig 62 and *see* Fig 67). Although he was unappreciated at home, there is an intriguing possibility that Ellis may have influenced the development of American high-rise offices: Oriel Chambers seems to anticipate the pioneering Chicago skyscrapers of John Wellborn Root, who was educated on Merseyside in the 1860s, where his uncle's office was a stone's throw from Ellis's recently completed building.

In general, windows became bigger and more numerous as the 19th century progressed. From at least the 1850s, sash windows were grouped together, divided only by slender cast-iron mullions supporting a continuous timber lintel, strengthened with iron. This sort of fenestration seems to have been confined to the less visible parts of buildings such as light wells, or to buildings in minor streets. From the 1860s, lintels of cast iron rather than timber were used, allowing more windows to be placed side by side in a continuous row, without compromising the strength of the wall. Picton did this in the block at the rear of the Temple, Dale Street (1863), and again on the side elevations of Fowler's Buildings, Victoria Street (1865–9; *see* Fig 22), where the windows are grouped in threes and

Figure 59 *Pekin Buildings, Harrington Street,* c*1859. [DP28724]*

Figure 60 (opposite) *Oriel Chambers, Water Street, 1864, by Peter Ellis. [AA030920]*

Figure 61 (above) *Glazed curtain walling to the courtyard elevation of Oriel Chambers, independent of the building's cast-iron frame. [DP28852]*

Figure 62 (left) *16 Cook Street, c1868, by Peter Ellis. [AA029108]*

fours, with chunky ironwork supplied by the local Union Foundry of Messrs R & J Rankin. At Gladstone Buildings in Union Court (c1877) as many as six windows are combined in strips 8m long (Fig 63), while at Percy Buildings in Eberle Street (c1878) the huge windows extend vertically from pavement to parapet through three storeys. Rows of windows under cast-iron lintels could also be inserted into older buildings to improve light levels, as appears to have happened at 6–8 Temple Court (Fig 64).

Figure 63 (below, left) *Multiple sash windows under cast-iron lintels at Gladstone Buildings, Union Court, c1877. [DP28729]*

Figure 64 (below, right) *6–8 Temple Court. [AA029109]*

Figure 65 (opposite) *The Cotton Exchange of 1905–6 by Matear & Simon. Cotton trading had traditionally taken place in the open air on the Exchange Flags, but with the growing commercial importance of the telephone towards the end of the 19th century, an indoor Cotton Exchange became necessary. Situated in Old Hall Street, it has a north elevation of prefabricated cast-iron panels, incorporating large windows to light the sample counters. [AA029477]*

The wider adoption of electricity from the 1890s does not seem to have lessened the demand for natural light, especially in the cotton trade, and Liverpool's most spectacular glazed façade belongs to Matear & Simon's Cotton Exchange, opened in 1906 (Fig 65). The north façade of this immense building is clad with Classically detailed cast-iron panels incorporating very large windows, expressly designed to light counters where cotton samples were examined. Nearby Orleans House in Edmund Street (1907) and City Buildings at the corner of Old Hall Street and Fazakerley Street (remodelled *c*1908; Fig 66) were both occupied by

Figure 66 (right) *City Buildings, Old Hall Street, remodelled c1908. [AA029116]*

cotton traders, and both use cast iron and broad expanses of glazing in the same way.

Fireproof construction, consisting of brick-vaulted floors carried on cast-iron columns, was used from the 1840s in some Liverpool warehouses, but it is not clear when the technology was first applied to office buildings. Some, such as Liverpool & London Chambers and Oriel Chambers, used it throughout, but in most cases the added expense was probably regarded as unjustifiable, and usually it seems to have been reserved for basement vaults, where highly flammable materials such as spirits might be stored. The parts of the building in office use generally had timber floors, though the safe or strong room belonging to each suite would be fireproof. For structural reasons, these small but very solidly constructed rooms would be positioned one above the other on each floor, rising through the building like a chimney stack. By the 1860s other methods of fireproof construction were in use. T H Wyatt's new Exchange Buildings of 1863–70 had concrete floors of a type devised by Messrs Fox & Barrett, but still they were confined to the ground floor and basement, used as bonded stores for flammable goods. In 1865 *The Builder* observed that

> Fire-proof flooring is much in esteem in Liverpool. It comes, perhaps, of a community of merchants that chances should be calculated to a nicety, and that all risk should be reduced to the minimum as far as expenditure can insure that desirability. In the court of the block of offices called the Temple … there are huge piles of offices in course of erection in white and red bricks, with iron girders to carry the floors and iron mullions to the window openings.[17]

What *The Builder* described at the Temple was not really fireproof construction, but simply the use of iron for certain components that would traditionally have been made of combustible timber. Peter Ellis employed cast iron instead of wood for the spiral staircase of 16 Cook Street in the mid-1860s (Fig 67), and by the 1880s cast-iron staircases were widely used. There are particularly impressive – and ornamental – examples at 14 Castle Street, Mersey Chambers and Union House.

With no building regulations to limit the height of office blocks, the main constraint in the first half of the 19th century was the absence of mechanical lifts. Hydraulic passenger lifts, raised and lowered by pressurised water, were in use in Liverpool by the 1860s – there was one in the rebuilt Exchange Buildings in 1866 – and by the early 1880s several office blocks such as Commercial Saleroom Buildings in Victoria Street and Central Buildings in North John Street had them. However, they became more efficient and more widespread from 1888, after the Liverpool Hydraulic Power Co introduced a system of high pressure water mains. In that year African Chambers in Old Hall Street became the first office building to have a passenger lift powered by the new company. Electricity was an alternative source of power, and after Liverpool Corporation took over the supply in 1896, its use for passenger

Figure 67 (right) *Cast-iron spiral staircase at 16 Cook Street, c1868. [DP28731]*

Figure 68 (far right) *Electric lift in the Municipal Buildings, Dale Street, probably installed in 1910. [DP28849]*

Figure 69 (opposite) *Royal Insurance building, corner of Dale Street and North John Street, 1896–1903, by James F Doyle. [AA040556]*

Figure 70 (below) *Section though Royal Insurance building, 1896–1903, by James F Doyle, showing the steel frame that supports the upper floors.* [From J Newby Hetherington, The Royal Insurance Company's Building, North John Street and Dale Street, Liverpool, *1903, Liverpool Record Office, Liverpool Libraries]*

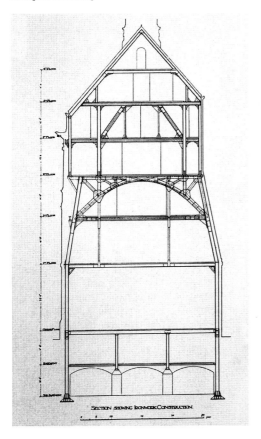

lifts seems gradually to have supplanted hydraulic power. The change was not instantaneous, however: from 1893 the Corporation's own Municipal Buildings had a hydraulic lift, which was not replaced by an electric one until 1910 (Fig 68). An early all-electric building was the General Post Office, completed in 1899. It had five electric lifts and was lit throughout by electricity, but power was generated on site rather than supplied from the mains.

Greater use of lifts was one reason why Liverpool office buildings became taller in the years around 1900. More important, however, was the use of framed construction, which meant that the weight of the floors could be borne by a framework of steel or reinforced concrete posts and beams, rather than external walls of expensive load-bearing masonry. Internal supporting walls could also be dispensed with, allowing more flexible planning. James F Doyle's Royal Insurance Building at the corner of Dale Street and North John Street (1896–1903, Fig 69) has one of the earliest self-sufficient steel frames in any British building (Fig 70). Contrary to appearance, it is this frame, not the external walls of rugged granite and Portland stone, that supports the upper storeys, leaving the huge public office that fills the ground floor completely free of columns. In the public office of the White Star Line building in James Street (1895–8, Fig 71) Richard Norman Shaw left riveted iron stanchions exposed to view, and in the former Parr's Bank, Castle Street (1898–1901, now NatWest; Fig 72), he used framed construction to support five floors of offices above the circular ground-floor banking hall. However, changes to building regulations were needed before external walls could be reduced to the thin cladding made possible by framed construction, and it was not until the Liverpool Corporation (General Powers) Act of 1908 that the benefits of the new technology could be fully exploited.

Liverpool's most ambitious pioneer of framed construction was Walter Aubrey Thomas. His Tower Buildings, begun in 1906, has a steel frame clad in white glazed terracotta (*see* Fig 7), and fireproof floors of reinforced hollow brickwork. It is surpassed in height by his Royal Liver Building of 1908–11 at the Pier Head, which has a reinforced concrete frame faced with granite, and a pair of extravagant towers that rise to

Figure 71 *Former public office of the White Star Line building, James Street, 1895–8, by Richard Norman Shaw; photographed in 1898 by Bedford Lemere. The ceiling is fireproof, of terracotta panels held in a cast-iron frame. [NMR BL 14773]*

Figure 72 *NatWest Bank (formerly Parr's Bank), Castle Street, 1898–1901, by Richard Norman Shaw with Willink & Thicknesse. [AA029151]*

90m (Figs 73 and 74). This was almost certainly the largest British office building of its day, and its monstrous scale, combined with its unique and exuberant silhouette, at once made it an unmistakable landmark. The towers are crowned with gigantic statues of mythical liver birds, symbols of the Royal Liver Friendly Society, the life assurance company that erected the building to house its headquarters. New technology allowed the Society to build on an unprecedented scale, but in doing so it was

Figure 73 (right) *Royal Liver Building, Pier Head, 1908–11, by Walter Aubrey Thomas. [AA017861]*

Figure 74 (below) *The Royal Liver Building under construction, showing the granite skin being attached to the reinforced concrete frame. [From* Concrete & Constructional Engineering, *6 (10), Oct 1911, Liverpool Libraries]*

Figure 75 *India Buildings, Water Street, 1923–30, by Arnold Thornely and Herbert J Rowse. [AA029202]*

simply following the same principles that shaped office blocks like Liverpool & London Chambers 50 years earlier: great size acted as an impressive advertisement for the firm, at the same time providing extensive lettable office space that generated rental income. In 1920, for example, the Royal Liver Friendly Society occupied only the eighth floor and part of the ground floor of its prestigious headquarters, while more than 120 other businesses occupied the rest as tenants.

No Liverpool office block topped the Royal Liver Building until the 1960s, but several very large steel-framed buildings went up in the early 20th century, giving an almost transatlantic character to the commercial centre. The most elegant are India Buildings (Fig 75) and Martins Bank Building (Fig 76), facing each other across the canyon of Water Street. Both were designed by Herbert J Rowse, who trained at the Liverpool School of Architecture before working for a period in Canada and the United States, and they show the clear influence of American commercial architecture in their enormous size and refined Italian Renaissance detailing. This influence was more strongly felt in the westward-looking port of Liverpool than in any other English city, and was vigorously promoted by the head of the Liverpool School of Architecture from 1904 to 1933, Charles Reilly. India Buildings shows the fullest development of the speculative office block in Liverpool. Incorporating a bank, post office, shopping arcade and underground railway access, it is an extraordinarily sophisticated descendant of George Holt's pioneering India Buildings, which first rose on part of the same site almost a century earlier.

Figure 76 *Martins Bank Building, Water Street, 1927–32, by Herbert J Rowse. [AA029204]*

CHAPTER 4

Servicing the commercial centre

These central spaces are left entirely at the disposal of … the clerk, the merchant and the broker … an agreeably apparelled army that gives a fine air of prosperity to all the streets.

D Scott 1907[18]

Office work was the main function of Liverpool's commercial district, but to meet the practical needs of the countless merchants and clerks, a complementary range of specialist businesses and services grew up.

Stationers and printers were very numerous, printing by letterpress or lithography being the only efficient way of copying documents in large quantities before the mid-20th century. They manufactured account books and produced the circulars, reports and forms that were vital to mercantile Liverpool. At 59–61 Tithebarn Street are the 1871 premises of the Union Paper and Printing Co, manufacturing and export stationers, with a vertical row of warehouse-style taking-in doors announcing their industrial purpose. More elegant is the building of Messrs Rockliff, publishers and printers, at 44 Castle Street, with a decorative 1880s faience façade worthy of its prestigious location (Fig 78); the printing works were at the back in Lower Castle Street. Elsewhere, printers were regularly to be found in the basements of office buildings, where the weight and vibration of the presses were likely to cause fewer problems than on upper floors. One of many was Thomas Brakell, who had premises in Imperial Chambers, Dale Street, extending back along Davies Street.

Everywhere there were cafés and restaurants, where office workers who commuted from increasingly distant suburbs could take their midday meal. A noted eating place in the 1850s was the now-demolished Merchants' Dining Rooms in Lancaster Buildings, Tithebarn Street, which was said to serve between 600 and 800 diners daily. The City Hall Restaurant in Eberle Street (now Garlands nightclub), reconstructed following a fire in 1879, was designed by Edmund Kirby for the leading caterer Philip Eberle, in whose honour the street was later renamed. Before the fire, it had an opulent interior with stained-glass roof lights in the large banqueting room, two billiard rooms, and several smaller bars and private dining rooms. Simpler facilities for the less affluent were

Figure 77 *The Royal Café and its staff, photographed in 1888 by Bedford Lemere. The café was in the basement of African Chambers, Old Hall Street, lit from above via a light well. [NMR BL08786]*

Figure 78 *44 Castle Street, former premises of Messrs Rockliff, printers.* [AA029155]

provided from 1884 by the Liverpool Clerks' Café Co, which had semi-basement premises in Ashcroft's Buildings, Victoria Street, in Central Buildings, North John Street, and in several other locations. As well as refreshments, they provided smoking rooms equipped with board games and operated a system by which diners could buy multiple meal vouchers at a discount. Many other semi-basements in office buildings were occupied by restaurants and cafés, such as the Royal Café, which had premises in African Chambers at 19 Old Hall Street (*see* Fig 77). A purpose-built example was the semi-basement of 1 Victoria Street, designed by Cornelius Sherlock for the brewer Andrew Barclay Walker, and now used as a pub. The nearby Lisbon in the same street has undergone the same change of use, but retains some of its late 19th-century decoration. The most splendid surviving restaurant interior occupies the ground floor of the former State Insurance building in Dale Street, its walls faced with polished green onyx, incorporating circular painted reliefs which depict nursery ballads.

Hotels provided overnight accommodation for business visitors, and in the 18th and early 19th centuries they were concentrated in Dale Street, the terminus for stagecoaches. Most have vanished, but a surviving stucco façade with giant Corinthian columns, opposite the end of Stanley Street, belongs to the former Grecian Hotel and apparently dates from *c*1829 (Fig 79). From the mid-19th century, railway stations became the new focus for travellers' accommodation, with the biggest hotels close to Lime Street Station and Central Station, outside the commercial centre. The rebuilt Exchange Station of the 1880s included a hotel, of which only the façade survives, and nearby at the corner of Tithebarn Street and Pall Mall is the former Bradford Hotel.

Political clubs were used for dining and for business meetings, and offered members facilities such as billiard rooms, reading rooms and some overnight accommodation (Fig 80 and *see* Fig 32). The Conservative, Reform and Junior Reform clubs all occupied imposing purpose-built premises on Dale Street, between the Exchange and the Municipal Buildings. Others, without explicit political affiliations, included the Liverpool in Moorfields, the Exchange at 11 Fenwick Street, and the Artists' in Percy Buildings, Eberle Street. Clubs for physical

Figure 79 *Façade of the former Grecian Hotel, Dale Street, c1829. [AA029164]*

Figure 80 *Reading room of the Conservative Club, Dale Street, photographed in 1888 by Bedford Lemere. [NMR BL08753]*

exercise and relaxation were also to be found near the Exchange, their late 20th-century proliferation in business districts belying a much longer history. A Turkish bath opened in Eberle Street in 1885, and Goad's 1888 insurance plans show a gymnasium in St George's Crescent and baths in the basement of an office building in North John Street.

Shops specialising in luxury goods for the wealthy (and invariably male) merchant class were naturally attracted to the central business district. By the late 19th century there was a concentration of tailors in North John Street, and in Central Buildings in the same street were the premises of the wine merchant James Smith, whose cellarage extended under the whole enormous block. Ashcroft's Buildings in Victoria Street was built in 1883 as the factory and showroom of James Ashcroft, a celebrated maker of billiard tables. The shop with elegant projecting display windows at 2 Castle Street was designed for the goldsmith Robert

Jones in 1882, while directly opposite, the former Exchange Art Gallery at 1 Castle Street was built in 1877 for the picture dealers Agnew's (Fig 81). Their previous premises were on the top floor of Liverpool & London Chambers, actually overlooking the Exchange Flags. Here, according to *The Porcupine* in 1866, they were able to 'blend Art and its antithesis – Trade – in a most marvellous manner' by offering for sale 'works of the very highest order … to the merchant princes'. [19]

Figure 81 *1 Castle Street, Agnew's Exchange Art Gallery (now the HSBC) with the British & Foreign Marine Insurance offices to the right. [AA029142]*

CHAPTER 5

Change, decline and legacy

The port's strategic importance made Liverpool a key target in the Second World War and bombing in the commercial centre caused widespread destruction, especially south of Lord Street and Derby Square (Fig 82 and *see* detail opposite). The greatest loss was the Custom House in Canning Place, which was gutted and afterwards demolished. Other badly damaged buildings, such as the White Star Line and India Buildings, were repaired more or less to their pre-war state, but the High Street façade of Liverpool & London Chambers still shows some scars. In the immediate post-war rebuilding the only really modern newcomer was the Corn Exchange in Brunswick Street, while elsewhere the Victorian and Edwardian *palazzo* tradition proved surprisingly tenacious, producing some solid, imposing office blocks faced in brick and stone, such as Reliance House in Water Street and Castle Chambers in Castle Street.

It was the 1960s and 1970s that really transformed the war-ravaged business district. The scale was set by 100 Old Hall Street, a 15-storey block begun in 1962, and the Liverpool City Centre Plan of 1965 earmarked the adjoining area north of the Exchange for further large-scale office expansion. Here a cluster of high-rise buildings, including Silkhouse Court and the Liverpool Daily Post and Echo, replaced a dense mass of 19th-century warehouses and offices. The ziggurat-like Royal & Sun Alliance headquarters (Fig 83) dominates, and shows the impact of artificial lighting and air-conditioning on late 20th-century office design: it has no light wells, and workstations in the middle of the lower floors are very far indeed from the narrow, arrow-slit windows, the exact opposite of arrangements in Oriel Chambers a century earlier. In the basement, where a 19th-century office block would have accommodated bonded warehousing, space is given over to car parking. Indeed, the car had become such a dominant presence by the 1960s that the City Centre Plan proposed a system of elevated walkways, to separate pedestrians from road traffic. Only disconnected fragments were ever constructed: surviving examples can be seen at Moorfields Station and at Kingsway House in Hatton Garden.

But the most radical change to emerge from the post-war decades was the obliteration of the 18th- and early 19th-century street

The Queen Victoria monument in 1944.

pattern south of Lord Street and Derby Square. Castle Street and its continuation, South Castle Street, had formed the spine of Liverpool, closed at the north end by the dome of the Town Hall and at the south end – from the 1820s – by the corresponding dome of the Custom House. The southward vista was cut off by the construction of the Queen Elizabeth II Law Courts, planned in 1973 and opened in 1984, across the path of South Castle Street, breaking the visual link with the historic site of the Pool. With the office towers of Old Hall Street to the north, the courts were meant to frame the Victorian commercial core when viewed from the river, an arrangement intended to preserve the famous skyline of the Pier Head and the two cathedrals on their distant ridge.

This period of ambitious redevelopment was short-lived, and dramatic economic decline from the 1970s began a quarter-century of stagnation and decay. The rise of air transport, the fading importance of empire, the emergence of continental Europe as Britain's main trading partner, and the decline of British manufacturing, especially the Lancashire cotton industry, all fatally undermined Liverpool's commercial role, accelerating trends that had been present since before the war. Shipping companies ceased operation or moved away, port-related trades closed down, and banks and insurance companies merged and transferred their head offices elsewhere. At the same time, Liverpool had to contend with changes common to all late 20th-century cities: cellular offices no longer met the needs of modern business, and

Figure 82 *The Queen Victoria monument, unscathed amid the devastation caused by air raids in 1941. In the distance is the ruin of the 1820s Custom House, minus its dome, closing the view down South Castle Street. [Photograph by Stewart Bale, 1944, courtesy of National Museums Liverpool, Merseyside Maritime Museum]*

Figure 83 *Royal & Sun Alliance, Old Hall Street, 1972–6, by Tripe & Wakeham. [AA040564]*

developments in information technology and private transport made out-of-town sites more attractive than the city centre.

Yet what remains, in spite of demolitions and some insensitive redevelopment, is a 19th- and early 20th-century commercial area of exceptional visual interest and historical importance. In the first decade of the 19th century – earlier than Glasgow, Manchester or Birmingham – Liverpool started to transform its historic centre into a dedicated business district. In contrast to the City of London, which shoehorned many of its Victorian commercial buildings into a maze of medieval streets, Liverpool created a rationally planned focus for its trading activities – the Exchange Buildings and the Flags – and gradually, over a period of 150 years, straightened and widened the surrounding thoroughfares into a dignified and functional grid. This street pattern gives coherence to an extremely varied collection of buildings, designed by architects of national standing as well as talented locals. Prosperity, competitiveness and enterprise are reflected in their costliness, diversity and sheer size, and in their imaginative use of new technologies and materials. Just as significant as the individual buildings, however, is the very existence of this clearly defined district, with its intricate network of office blocks, commodity exchanges and financial institutions. Unlike the more diffuse commercial centres of other Victorian cities, it points to the vital importance, from an early date, of Liverpool's office-based economy, and it embodies the workings of a great mercantile city at the height of Britain's industrial strength.

CHAPTER 6

Conserving the commercial centre

In July 2004 much of Liverpool's waterfront, warehouse district, cultural quarter and historic commercial centre was inscribed as a UNESCO World Heritage Site. The inscription acknowledges the sheer quality of the cityscape and the exceptional testimony that it bears to the development of global trade and commerce. However, the story that has unfolded in preceding chapters is not that of a museum piece but of the heart of a vibrant metropolis, pulsating with activity and confidence. Liverpool has been through turbulent times but remains one of the UK's major cities and retains a significant international profile. The city centre is the driver of a large sub-regional economy. As it engages in a dramatic process of regeneration and redevelopment, the task is to harness the confidence and innovation with which the city has long been synonymous. New life needs to be injected into Liverpool's commercial heart in a manner that reinforces the qualities which make it so special.

Cities are not static but are constantly evolving. They are dynamic places that must respond to shifting circumstance and meet the changing needs and aspirations of successive generations. Liverpool has had to adapt more than most, its hand being forced by a spectacular economic decline. In a few short decades the trade and commerce which formed Liverpool's essence, and which the cityscape had been so perfectly constructed to serve, was all but wiped out.

The magnitude of the change that engulfed the country in the post-war period was unprecedented. In cities everywhere 19th-century townscapes were viewed as outdated and an uncomfortable reminder of a different era. Radical solutions were sought, dramatic gestures that would deliver the cities of tomorrow. Yet while others busied themselves with demolition and the creation of a new urban form, Liverpool's declining resources prevented it from fully realising the 1965 City Centre Plan with its network of 'streets in the sky'. The retention of much of the outstanding historic cityscape was an unforeseen consequence of faltering fortunes, and this landscape is now one of Liverpool's greatest assets.

The legacy of post-war town planning and the dominance of the motor car have led to a re-examination of the environments in which we live and work. Successive governments have sought to encourage a renaissance of our towns and cities through the development of people-friendly places. Liverpool's historic commercial centre exemplifies much of what is now regarded as urban design best practice and 'place-making'. As an environment developed specifically to support face-to-face transactions, the commercial centre caters for the experience of the individual rather than the motor car. Buildings on a human scale; streets enlivened by shops and restaurants; high-quality public realm; clearly identified entrances; ground-floor spaces that welcome and inspire; landmark public buildings; a hierarchy of pedestrian routes; and a distinct sense of place: all have become accepted principles of good urban design. Concepts such as 'mixed use' are currently being heavily promoted but were simply a commercial reality to our forebears. The provision of retail units at street level and letting of basements to services and catering establishments were just common sense to a 19th-century speculative office developer. Once viewed as outmoded, the historic townscape is now generally regarded as a benchmark for new development elsewhere within Liverpool city centre.

Despite a renewed appreciation of its qualities and international significance, the commercial centre still faces considerable challenges. Liverpool is no longer the hub of a global trading network and an international financial centre. With a number of notable exceptions, the shipping companies, insurance houses, commodity exchanges and banks have moved on. The long-term effects of low property values and neglect have taken their toll on the physical fabric (Fig 84).

The city's recent and still relatively fragile rejuvenation has involved remarkable levels of investment and rekindled development interest within the historic commercial centre (Fig 85). But these are still the early stages of what needs to be a sustained process of regeneration if the effects of past decades are to be reversed. There have been fundamental changes to business practice and the wider economy, and the forms of activity now competing for space are often very different from their predecessors. Much of the physical fabric requires substantial sums to be spent on it to combat the effects of past neglect and provide appropriate accommodation for potential new uses. The commercial centre must adapt to take advantage of changing fortunes but must

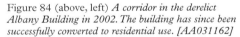

Figure 84 (above, left) *A corridor in the derelict Albany Building in 2002. The building has since been successfully converted to residential use. [AA031162]*

Figure 85 (above, right) *The interior of the Albany Building in 2007. [Joseph Sharples]*

do so in a manner that retains and reinforces the distinct qualities recognised by UNESCO.

World Heritage Site status places responsibilities on the UK government to ensure that the 'outstanding universal value' of the site is understood, sustained and communicated. However, it does not in itself bring any specific form of protection, but instead relies upon existing mechanisms provided by the English planning system. These have been developed to conserve buildings and areas of 'special architectural or historic interest'. Many buildings in the commercial centre are individually listed, affording statutory protection for both their external appearance and internal layout and detailing. But much of the area's significance lies in the relationship between the buildings, and Liverpool

City Council has consequently included most of the commercial district within the Castle Street Conservation Area.

The World Heritage Site Management Plan acknowledges that the best way to conserve the site is to ensure that it is actively used. This means encouraging the sensitive adaptation of buildings to accommodate the needs of current and proposed occupants while preserving their essential characteristics. In the case of some commercial centre office buildings, it may be difficult to meet modern requirements. The need within refurbished historic buildings for disability access and systems of fire prevention, heating, information technology and sanitation tests the design skills of the architect and engineer. In most cases a considered approach can lead to a solution. Reliance House and India Buildings on Water Street show how a subtle use can be made of the existing topography to provide wheelchair access to main entrances (Fig 86).

Changes to the local economy and business practices have reduced the demand for cellular office accommodation. The construction of large floor plate buildings beyond the traditional boundaries of the commercial core has gradually shifted the centre of gravity away from Victoria Street and Dale Street. Changes to local infrastructure have released desirable new sites, such as Princes Dock, for the construction of the types of commercial properties now called for. The redevelopment of St Paul's Square and imminent development of what amounts to an entire new city-centre quarter on land formerly occupied by Exchange Station and its approaches will draw the focus of commercial activities even further north. The properties left behind have had to find alternative occupants.

Many owners and developers have seen an opportunity to meet the growing demand for city-centre living. The robust nature of the office buildings, with their generous internal spaces and good access to the natural light needed by merchants, makes them well suited to careful adaptation. The more functional warehouse buildings on the narrow streets to the rear have raised difficult design issues, but award-winning schemes such as Preston Point in Preston Street and the Old Haymarket demonstrate how a successful conversion can retain the integrity and interest of the building. This is a topic addressed in greater detail in the

Figure 86 *India Buildings, Water Street where the natural slope of the ground is exploited to aid wheelchair access. [Joseph Sharples]*

companion publication *Storehouses of Empire: Liverpool's Historic Warehouses* (2004).

It is not only historic buildings that have had to change. Adaptability is a key consideration for all forms of development. In recent years many of the post-war structures that were part of the radical vision of a new Liverpool have undergone substantial alteration. The former City Council planning department of Wilberforce House has been reinvented as Beetham Plaza, a residential development with a glazed restaurant extension at ground-floor level, providing animation to the adjacent public square (Fig 87). Similarly, the Royal & Sun Alliance (recently rebranded The Capital) and Liverpool Daily Post and Echo, both modern

Figure 87 (opposite) *Restaurant, Beetham Plaza: an imaginative addition to a dull 1960s office building.* *[AA029339]*

office towers, have replaced a confusing network of vehicular ramps and walkways with City Exchange, a glazed atrium that provides access to both buildings and a clear frontage to Old Hall Street (Fig 88). Although constructed in glass and steel, this sort of airy semi-public environment recaptures some of the basic qualities of a traditional top-lit banking hall.

During leaner times, developments were permitted that retained merely the shells of buildings within the commercial centre. This literally superficial approach may have been born out of economic necessity, but it ignored the fact that the qualities of the commercial centre are based on more than the façades of its buildings. It is often the accumulation of what at first appear to be minor incidental details that creates rich layers of interest.

Homebuyers and commercial occupants are placing an increasing emphasis on individual character and style. The retention of fine-grain features helps to emphasise the unique qualities of a property, increasing its potential desirability. As part of the conversion of the Albany to residential use, the ornate gates on the main entrance have been restored and a glass screen carefully inserted to keep out the worst effects of the weather. Elsewhere, tiled entrances to former office buildings provide characterful and robust circulation spaces in residential conversions. Wall-mounted hoists, such as can be found on Sweeting Street and Ormond Street, are a lingering reminder of a building's former use. Loading bays on warehouses, like those to the rear of 73–89 Victoria Street, create opportunities for valuable external space in the form of balconies. These unique features can add a premium to a development, but if not given appropriate consideration they can all too easily be lost, and the character of the area permanently diminished.

The ground floors of buildings are particularly vulnerable to insensitive alteration. As any visitor to the former Martins Bank on Water Street will be aware, the city's banking halls and public lobbies can be spaces of real scale and drama which would be difficult to replicate today (*see* Fig 54). Some of the grandest halls, such as the former Lloyds Bank in India Buildings, have only relatively recently been subdivided to provide additional office space, while a number of others, including the former Royal Insurance on North John Street, remain vacant

Figure 88 *City Exchange, Old Hall Street, completed 2001, by KKA. [DP34001]*

and inaccessible. However, examples such as New Zealand House in Water Street (Fig 89) and the former Alliance Bank at 62 Castle Street demonstrate how these opulent spaces can potentially find a prosperous future as the new social arenas of a growing city-centre residential community.

There has been a strong revival in the food, drink and retail establishments that were once such a vital part of the commercial centre. Active ground floors help to animate the street scene, but such are the demands of corporate branding that a proliferation of standardised shopfronts can also erode the unique sense of place. Fortunately, here

Figure 89 *New Zealand House, Water Street. The large spaces in some 19th-century commercial buildings lend themselves successfully to leisure uses. [Photograph courtesy of Newzbar]*

Figure 90 *Shopfront, 52 Castle Street. [DP28730]*

too, character is increasingly being viewed as an asset to the business, often by some of the larger international concerns. Bang & Olufsen (Fig 90) and Starbucks, at 52 and 2 Castle Street respectively, and Reiss on Mathew Street (Fig 91), are among those that embrace the qualities of the host building as a positive element of their identity. The success of these types of establishment has greatly increased the variety within the commercial centre and extended the period of activity well beyond office hours.

It is not only shopfronts that reflect powerful brands: whole buildings have been conceived to reinforce corporate identity. This is not a new phenomenon, as is exemplified by Alfred Waterhouse's series of late 19th-century offices for the Prudential Assurance Co, including the branch in Dale Street. But where Waterhouse adopted a housestyle to create highly individual buildings attuned to their settings, modern methods of construction are now able to deliver a standardised kit of parts. For some businesses there has been a temptation to harness this potential and make virtues of familiarity and sameness. Such an approach would sit uncomfortably within the commercial centre, where the nature of the townscape demands a specific response to the particular

Figure 91 *Reiss, a fashion store in a converted 19th-century office building in Mathew Street. The new entrance matches the scale of the original building, and its narrow proportions echo the warehouse loading bays of neighbouring blocks. [DP28722]*

characteristics of the site. The Travelodge on Manchester Street provides an example of the housestyle being set aside in favour of a strikingly modern structure designed in response to its local surroundings.

Amid the flurry of building activity that has overtaken much of central Liverpool, there remain a limited number of empty sites and redevelopment opportunities within the commercial centre. They do not call for a pastiche of historic architectural styles, which would be at odds with the spirit of an area synonymous with innovation and flair. The latest styles, materials and technologies have consistently been embraced and skilfully articulated in a manner that takes cues from neighbouring buildings and the wider townscape. There is a basic underlying order which, like an unspoken set of rules, has been politely observed or modified over time. Some of these 'rules', like the relatively consistent building height in areas such as Dale Street, are a consequence of technological constraints. Others, including the widths of the main thoroughfares, were part of a deliberate plan. But most were a basic response to functional needs. Regardless of their derivation, these tacit guidelines enable a diverse range of buildings to form a coherent townscape.

The current generation of tall residential developments is challenging the relatively consistent building height in the commercial centre. Limited additional height can sometimes be accommodated by stepping upper storeys back. Martins Bank Building (1927–32, *see* Fig 76) is an early example. Additional value is increasingly being sought from refurbishment projects by incorporating additional floors arranged in this manner. The addition of lightweight penthouse structures is a feature of the refurbishment of the former parcel sorting office on Hatton Garden and the residential scheme at Old Haymarket. In both cases the extra accommodation sits comfortably on top of the original structure. However, the impact of such additions on the character of the building and its surroundings can be considerable, particularly in medium and long-distance views.

The impact of tall buildings depends not only on location and context, but on design quality too. Architects of Liverpool's earliest tall commercial structures were interested in much more than just eye-catching height. For the Royal Insurance building J F Doyle used superb materials, including huge, rugged granite blocks for the ground floor. He gave the upper storeys a magnificent carved frieze, and created a dramatic skyline by combining a gold-domed tower with a parade of massive chimney stacks. In the Royal Liver Building, Walter Aubrey Thomas produced a landmark of memorable individuality that has become an instantly recognisable symbol of the city. In these historical examples attention to detail, quality of materials and above all inventiveness are just as important as height; the same principles applied to the current wave of development may well produce a new generation of buildings of which the city can be proud.

There is undoubtedly a place for high-quality tall buildings within
Liverpool city centre and they will mark a further stage in the city's
continued evolution. Despite the economic success of recent years
there remains considerable scope for redevelopment and exciting new
additions to the urban form. A number of potential sites where tall
structures could be grouped have been suggested. One such area is north
of the collection of large-scale developments built around Old Hall Street
in the 1960s and 1970s. A cluster of tall structures here may play an
important part in defining the character of a new business district and
make a welcome addition to Liverpool's distinctive skyline.

The scale of new development is the latest challenge facing
Liverpool's commercial centre, but this should be welcomed: it shows
that economic regeneration is actually happening. The goal must be
to manage this process carefully, and to ensure that having survived
both the destructive zeal of redevelopment in the 1960s and 1970s and
the gradual decay that followed, the architectural legacy of the city's
commercial heyday is reinvigorated rather than compromised. There
remains the danger of incremental erosion through the loss of fine-grain
features and the cumulative impact of poorly conceived additions. There
are also some major issues to resolve, such as finding appropriate uses
for existing buildings requiring substantial investment. However, this
would be expected in any regenerating city. What is important is that
this area of 'outstanding universal value' remains a vibrant and successful
part of one of England's great cities. With sensitive management, allied
to a recognition of changing requirements, it can thrive for the benefit of
future generations, both in Liverpool and the wider global community.

Notes

1 Kohl, J G 1844 *England and Wales*. Reprinted 1968, London: Frank Cass, 41

2 Walker, P [W Allingham] 1873 *Rambles*. London, 214–5

3 Troughton, T 1810 *The History of Liverpool*. Liverpool, 333

4 Picton 1873, 2 269–70

5 Owen, J 1921 *The Cotton Broker*. London: Hodder & Stoughton, 217

6 'Brother Sam in Water Street'. *Liverpool Review* **17**, 11 Dec 1886, 6

7 'The Social Science Association and Liverpool'. *The Builder* **16**, 23 Oct 1858, 705–6

8 Liverpool Record Office, 352 MIN/IMP I 1/1, 27 Jun 1786

9 Liverpool Record Office, 920 DUR 2/16/7; draft letter from Holt to Chairman of Finance Committee, 20 Jul 1833

10 Whitty 1871, 35

11 Herdman and Picton 1864, 33

12 Maritime Archives, Merseyside Maritime Museum, DX/1477; transcript of S*ketch of the Commercial Life of H E Stripe*

13 Ellison 1905, 300

14 'Empty offices'. *The Porcupine* **10**, 9 May 1868, 60

15 'Improvements in Liverpool: architectural'. *The Porcupine* **10**, 5 Dec 1868, 349

16 'The Exchange Buildings, Liverpool'. *The Builder* **28**, 12 Feb 1870, 119–20

17 'A lounge in Liverpool'. *The Builder* **23**, 4 Nov 1865, 776

18 Scott, 1907, 78–9

19 'Mr. Leighton's last picture'. *The Porcupine* **8**, 24 Nov 1866, 401

References and further reading

Books

Ellison, T 1905 *Gleanings & Reminiscences*. Liverpool: Henry Young & Sons

Giles, C and Hawkins, B 2004 *Storehouses of Empire: Liverpool's Historic Warehouses*. London: English Heritage

Herdman, W and Picton, J A 1864 *Views in Modern Liverpool*. Liverpool: Marples

Picton, J A 1873 *Memorials of Liverpool*, 2 vols, London

Scott, D 1907 *Liverpool, Painted by J. Hamilton Hay, Described by Dixon Scott*. London: A & C Black

Sharples, J 2004 *Liverpool*. New Haven and London: Yale University Press

Whitty's Guide to Liverpool 1871

Archival sources

Correspondence of George Holt relating to India Buildings, Liverpool Record Office, 920 DUR 2/16/1–13

Culshaw and Sumners papers, Lancashire Record Office, Preston, DDX 162

Transcript of *Sketch of the Commercial Life of H E Stripe*, Maritime Archives, Merseyside Maritime Museum, DX/1477

Liverpool titles in the Informed Conservation series

Building a Better Society: Liverpool's historic institutional buildings. Colum Giles, 2008. Product code 51332, ISBN 9781873592908

Built on Commerce: Liverpool's central business district. Joseph Sharples and John Stonard, 2008. Product code 51331, ISBN 9781905624348

Ordinary Landscapes, Special Places: Anfield, Breckfield and the growth of Liverpool's suburbs. Adam Menuge, 2008. Product code 51343, ISBN 9781873592892

Places of Health and Amusement: Liverpool's historic parks and gardens. Katy Layton-Jones and Robert Lee, 2008. Product code 51333, ISBN 9781873592915

Religion and Place: Liverpool's historic places of worship. Sarah Brown and Peter de Figueiredo, 2008. Product code 51334, ISBN 9781873592885

Storehouses of Empire: Liverpool's historic warehouses. Colum Giles and Bob Hawkins, 2004. Product code 50920, ISBN 9781873592809

Other titles in this series

Behind the Veneer: The South Shoreditch furniture trade and its buildings. Joanna Smith and Ray Rogers, 2006. Product code 51204, ISBN 9781873592960

The Birmingham Jewellery Quarter: An introduction and guide. John Cattell and Bob Hawkins, 2000. Product code 50205, ISBN 9781850747772

Bridport and West Bay: The buildings of the flax and hemp industry. Mike Williams, 2006. Product code 51167, ISBN 9781873592861

Built to Last? The buildings of the Northamptonshire boot and shoe industry. Kathryn A Morrison with Ann Bond, 2004. Product code 50921, ISBN 9781873592793

Gateshead: Architecture in a changing English urban landscape. Simon Taylor and David Lovie, 2004. Product code 52000, ISBN 9781873592762

Manchester's Northern Quarter. Simon Taylor and Julian Holder, 2008. Product code 50946, ISBN 9781873592847

Manchester: The warehouse legacy – An introduction and guide. Simon Taylor, Malcolm Cooper and P S Barnwell, 2002. Product code 50668, ISBN 9781873592670

Margate's Seaside Heritage. Nigel Barker, Allan Brodie, Nick Dermott, Lucy Jessop and Gary Winter, 2007. Product code 51335, ISBN 9781905624669

Newcastle's Grainger Town: An urban renaissance. Fiona Cullen and David Lovie, 2003. Product code 50811, ISBN 9781873592779

'One Great Workshop': The buildings of the Sheffield metal trades. Nicola Wray, Bob Hawkins and Colum Giles, 2001. Product code 50214, ISBN 9781873592663

Religion and Place in Leeds. John Minnis and Trevor Mitchell, 2007. Product code 51337, ISBN 9781905624485

Stourport-on-Severn: Pioneer town of the canal age. Colum Giles, Keith Falconer, Barry Jones and Michael Taylor. Product code 51290, ISBN 9781905624362

£7.99 each (plus postage and packing)

To order tel: EH Sales 01761 452966
Email: ehsales@gillards.com
Online bookshop: www.english-heritage.org.uk

The commercial centre, showing buildings mentioned in the text

KEY

1   100 Old Hall Street

2   Bradford Hotel

3   59–61 Tithebarn Street

4   Tramway Offices

5   Kingsway House

6   135–9 Dale Street

7   Magistrates' Courts, Bridewell & Fire Station

8   Queensway Tunnel Entrance

9   Travelodge, Old Haymarket, Preston Point

10 Victoria Chapel

11 Princes Building

12 Grecian Hotel

13 Musker's Building (Junior Reform Club)

14 Imperial Chambers

15 Conservative Club

16 Granite Buildings

17 Ashcroft's Building

18 Lisbon Buildings

19 Union House

20 Victoria Buildings

21 Fowler's Buildings

22 Met Quarter (former GPO)

23 Commercial Saleroom Buildings

24 Fruit Exchange

25 Produce Exchange Buildings

26 Reiss

27 Kansas Buildings

28 Central Buildings

29 62 Castle Street (former Alliance Bank)

30 North and South Wales Bank

31 Beetham Plaza

32 White Star Line

33 Site of 17 James Street

34 Queen Victoria Monument (site of castle)

35 Queen Elizabeth II Law Courts

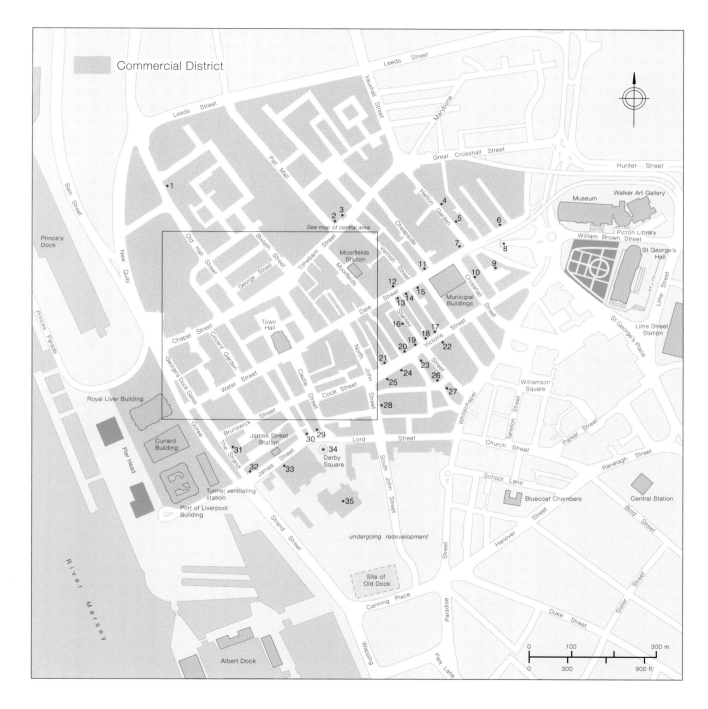

Commercial District

Detail of the area around the Exchange Flags

KEY

36 Liverpool Daily Post and Echo	65 Mersey Chambers
37 Orleans House	66 Tower Buildings
38 Royal and Sun Alliance	67 Reliance House
39 City Exchange	68 New Zealand House
40 Cotton Exchange	69 Oriel Chambers
41 City Buildings	70 India Buildings
42 7 Union Street	71 2 Castle Street
43 Tunnel ventilating tower	72 1 Castle Street
44 Rumford Court	73 British and Foreign Marine Insurance Co
45 African Chambers	
46 Albany Building	74 Queen Arcade
47 Windsor Buildings	75 Royal Bank
48 Berey's Buildings	76 Royal Bank Buildings
49 Mercury Court (former Exchange Station)	77 State Insurance
	78 Tunnel ventilating tower
50 The Railway public house	79 1 Victoria Street
51 Silkhouse Court	80 Gladstone Buildings
52 Messers Rowlinson's, Tempest Hey	81 14 Castle Street
53 City Hall Restaurant	82 NatWest Bank (former Parr's Bank)
54 Percy Buildings	
55 Reform Club	83 27 Castle Street
56 Prudential Assurance	84 Bank of England
57 The Temple	85 16 Cook Street
58 Royal Insurance	86 Harrington Chambers
59 11 Dale Street	87 Pekin Buildings
60 Mason's Building	88 Castle Chambers
61 Exchange Buildings	89 44 Castle Street
62 Liverpool and London Insurance Co	90 52 Castle Street
63 Martins Bank Building	91 Heywood's Bank
64 Hargreaves Buildings	92 Corn Exchange

Back cover
Keystone, Cunard Building, Pier Head, 1914–16.
[DP034128]